I0119384

John B. Pine

Charters, Acts and Official Documents

Together with the lease and re-lease by Trinity church of a portion of the King's

farm

John B. Pine

Charters, Acts and Official Documents
Together with the lease and re-lease by Trinity church of a portion of the King's farm

ISBN/EAN: 9783743407305

Manufactured in Europe, USA, Canada, Australia, Japa

Cover: Foto ©ninafisch / pixelio.de

Manufactured and distributed by brebook publishing software
(www.brebook.com)

John B. Pine

Charters, Acts and Official Documents

Columbia College
in the City of New York

CHARTERS
ACTS AND OFFICIAL DOCUMENTS

TOGETHER WITH THE

LEASE AND RE-LEASE BY TRINITY CHURCH
OF A PORTION OF THE
KING'S FARM

COMPILED BY

JOHN B. PINE

CLERK OF THE TRUSTEES

New York

PRINTED FOR THE COLLEGE

JUNE, 1895

Table of Contents.

Charters, Acts and Official Documents.

ACTS RELATING TO THE COLLEGE.

AN ACT FOR RAISING THE SUM OF TWO THOUSAND TWO HUN-
DRED AND FIFTY POUNDS BY A PUBLICK LOTTERY FOR THIS
COLONY FOR THE ADVANCEMENT OF LEARNING AND TOWARDS THE
FOUNDING OF A COLLEGE WITHIN THE SAME.

PASSED DECEMBER 6, 1746.

LAWS OF 1746, CHAP. 840.

Recites that "Inasmuch as it will greatly tend to the welfare
and reputation of the colony that a proper and ample foundation be laid for the regular education of youth, and as so good
and laudable a design must readily excite the inhabitants of this
colony to become adventurers in a lottery of which the profits
shall be employed for the founding of a colledge for that purpose;" and provides for erecting a lottery, appointing Peter
Vallete and Peter Van Brugh Livingston as managers. The Act
specifies in detail the manner in which the lottery shall be managed and impowers the Mayor, Recorder, Aldermen and Commonalty of the City of New York to inspect the same, and after
authorizing the managers to retain fifteen per cent. for their fees
and expenses, directs that the balance of the moneys arising
from the lottery be paid "into the hands of the Treasurer, to
be and remain in the Treasury, to and for the purpose of founding a colledge, for the education of youth, and to and for no
other purpose whatsoever, in such manner as shall be hereafter directed by act or acts of the Governor, Council and
General Assembly." The act further provides "that the purpose of founding the said colledge may not be obstructed by

any other application of the moneys to arise from the profits
of the said lottery, be it enacted by the authority aforesaid,
that each and every representative in General Assembly for the
time being, who shall hereafter in General Assembly, move or
consent to the applying or appropriating the said moneys to any
other purpose whatever, than the founding the colledge aforesaid, shall be and hereby is declared and made forever incapable
of sitting and voting in this or any future General Assembly,
and new writs shall issue accordingly."

An Act for Raising the Sum of One thousand Eight Hundred Pounds by a Publick Lottery for a further Provision
towards founding a College for the Advancement of Learning within this Colony.   Passed April 8, 1748.
                              Laws of 1748, Chap. 860.

Contains recitals and provisions similar to the foregoing act
passed December 6, 1746, and directs that the balance of the
moneys arising from the lottery, after deducting fifteen per
cent. for expenses, be paid to the Treasurer "to and for the
purpose of founding a college for the education of youths and
to and for no other purpose whatever."

An Act to Revive an Act entituled An Act for raising the
Sum of Eighteen hundred Pounds by a Publick Lottery for
a further Provision towards founding a College for the
Advancement of Learning within this Colony, with an
Addition thereto.   Passed October 28, 1748.
                              Laws of 1748, Chap. 870.

The time for raising the sum specified in the foregoing act,
passed April 9, 1748, having expired in September, for want of
a sufficient number of contributions, the said act was revived,
and the time for the drawing of the lottery as therein provided
was extended to November 14.

AN ACT FOR VESTING IN TRUSTEES THE SUM OF THREE THOU-
SAND FOUR HUNDRED AND FORTY-THREE POUNDS, EIGHTEEN
SHILLINGS, RAISED BY WAY OF A LOTTERY FOR ERECTING A COL-
LEGE WITHIN THIS COLONY.   PASSED NOVEMBER 25, 1751.
LAWS OF 1751, CHAP. 909.

Recites that " Whereas the sum of three thousand four hundred and forty-three pounds, eighteen shillings, has been raised
within this colony, by way of lottery, for erecting a College for
the education of youths within the same; which sum being not
conceived sufficient, without further addition, to answer the
said end of erecting, compleating & establishing a college for
the advancement of useful learning, it is conceived necessary
that Trustees be appointed, as well for the setting at interest
the said sum of three thousand four hundred and forty-three
pounds, eighteen shillings, already raised for the said purpose, as for receiving the contributions and donations of such
persons as may be charitably disposed to be benefactors and
encouragers of so laudable an undertaking," and appoints
as Trustees " the eldest Councellor residing in this Colony,
the Speaker of the General Assembly, and the Judges of the
Supreme Court, the Mayor of the City of New York, the
Treasurer of this Colony for the time being, together with
James Livingston, Esq., Mr. Benjamin Nicoll and Mr.
William Livingston," with power to manage the said sum and
additional contributions, and to receive proposals from any of
the cities or counties within this colony, desirous of having the
said college erected therein.

AN ACT FURTHER TO CONTINUE THE DUTY OF EXCISE, AND THE
CURRENCY OF THE BILLS OF CREDIT EMITTED THEREON, FOR THE
PURPOSES IN THE FORMER ACT, AND HEREIN MENTIONED.
PASSED JULY 4, 1753.
LAWS OF 1753, CHAP. 12.

The Act provides for various duties and authorizes the payment
by the Treasurer of the Colony to the Trustees mentioned and

appointed in and by the foregoing Act passed November 25, 1751, the annual sum of five hundred pounds, for the term of seven years, for the payment of salaries and for such other "uses and purposes concerning the establishment of the said Seminary" as the Trustees think needful.

AN ACT FOR RAISING THE SUM OF ONE THOUSAND ONE HUNDRED AND TWENTY-FIVE POUNDS, BY A PUBLICK LOTTERY FOR THIS COLONY FOR A FURTHER PROVISION TOWARDS FOUNDING A COLLEGE WITHIN THE SAME.   PASSED DECEMBER 12, 1753.
LAWS OF 1753, CHAP. 17.

Contains recitals and provisions similar to those contained in the Acts passed December 6, 1746, and April 9, 1748, and appoints as managers, Abraham Van Wyck and Abraham Leynsen, Esquires. The Act also provides that the proceeds of the lottery, after the payment of expenses, shall be paid to the Trustees appointed in and by the Act passed November 25, 1751, "and by them put out at Interest according to the directions of the said Act untill the same shall be employed by some Future Act for and towards founding a College for the advancement of learning within this Colony."

PETITION FOR A CHARTER.

To the Honourable James DeLancey Esqr. Lieutenant Governor and Commander in Chief of the Province of New York, and Territories-thereon depending in America. In Council

The Petition of the Trustees mentioned and appointed in by An Act, passed in the twenty fifth year of his present Majesty's Reign, Entituled An Act for vesting in Trustees the Sum of Three Thousand four hundred and forty-three pounds eighteen shillings, raised by way of Lottery for erecting a Colledge within this Colony. HUMBLY SHEWETH.

That divers Sums of money having been raised by several Acts of the Governor, Council, and General Assembly of this of New York, for the establishing a Colledge in the said province Your petitioners by Acts afterwards made, were appointed Trustees for putting the said Moneys at Interest, and to receive proposals, accept Donations, and procure Masters and Tutors, in order to make a Beginning of the said Seminary according to the trust reposed in them.

Your Petitioners further shew unto your Honour, That in pursuance of the said Trust, they have endeavoured to get a proper Master and Tutor for the said intended Seminary, But find that as your Petitioners, are enabled to give Salarys for seven years only, that they are under great difficulty to procure a fit and proper person to undertake the office of master or head of the said Seminary: Your petitioners further shew unto your Honour, that the Rector and Inhabitants of the City of New York in Communion of the Church of England as by Law established, being willing to encourage the said Good design of establishing a Seminary or College for the education of Youth, in the Liberal Arts or Sciences, have offered unto your Petitioners, a very valuable parcel of Ground on the west side of the Broadway, in the west ward of the City of New York, for the use of the said intended Seminary or College, and are ready and desirous to convey the said Lands for the said use, on Condition that the

7

head or Master of the said Seminary or Colledge, be a Member of and in Communion with the Church of England as by Law Established, and that the Liturgy of the said Church or a Collection of prayers out of the said Liturgy, be the constant morning and evening service, used in the said College forever, which said parcel of Land so offered by the said Rector and Inhabitants, your Petitioners considering as the most proper place for erecting of the said Seminary or College upon, and that their obtaining his Majesty's Charter to them or such others as your Honour shall think proper for the said Trust, will the better enable your petitioners in conjunction with those your Honour shall incorporate by his Majesty's Charter, to provide a proper Master, or head of the said Seminary, and Tutors for the Education of Youth, and thereby greatly tend to promote and further the intent and design of establishing a Seminary or College for the Education of Youth among us.

Your Petitioners therefore humbly pray, that in order to promote so good a design, and the more effectual obtaining a grant of the said parcel of Land for the use and benefit of the said Seminary or College, that your Honour would be pleased to grant to your Petitioners, or to such other persons as your Honour shall think proper, his Majesty's Charter of Incorporation, with such privileges as to your Honour shall seem meet, the better to enable them to prosecute the said design of Establishing a Seminary or College for the Instruction of Youth.

And your Petitioners shall ever pray.

New York, May 20th, 1754.   WM. LIVINGSTON
                    by order of the Trustees.

WARRANT TO PREPARE A CHARTER.

By the Hon. James DeLancey Esq., his Majesties Lieut. Gov. & Com. in Chief in & over the province of New York and the territories depending thereon in America

To William Kempe Esq his Majesties Attorney General for the province of New York

Whereas the Trustees mentioned & appointed in and by an act passed in the twenty-fifth of his Majesties Reign for vesting in the said Trustees Sum £3443:18 raised by way of a lottery for erecting a College within this Colony hath by their humble Petition presented unto me and had in Council on the 28th day of May last humby prayed I would grant to them the petitioners or to such persons as should be thought proper his Majesties Charter of Incorporation with such privileges as should be thought meet Which Petition was then referred to a Committee of the Gentlemen of the Council or any five of them. The Chairman whereof afterwards reported that the Committee was humbly of the Opinion that I should grant to proper persons his Majesties Letters Patent for incorporating the said College according to the purport and prayer of the petition and direct the attorney General to prepare a draft of the said Letters Patent or Charter Which report was agreed to and approved of as by the said petition and the proceedings in council thereupon copies of which are hereunto annexed may more fully and at large appear.

I have theretofore thought it Good with the advice of his Majesties Council to direct & you are hereby directed & required to prepare a draft of the said Letters Patent or Charter according to the purport and prayer of the said petition and to lay the same before me in Council And for so doing this shall be your sufft warrant.

Given under my Hand and Seal of Arms at Fort George in the City of New York this fourth day of June one thousand seven hundred & fifty-four.

THE CHARTER OF The Governors of the College of the Province of New York in the City of New York in America.

George the Second, by the grace of God, of Great Britain, France, and Ireland, King, Defender of the Faith, &c. *To all whom* these presents shall come, *Greeting:*

Whereas, by several acts of the Governour, Council, and General assembly of our Province of New York, divers sums of money have been Raised by Publick Lotteries, and appropriated for the founding, erecting, and establishing a College in our said Government, for the Education and Instruction of Youth in the Liberal Arts and Sciences:

And Whereas, the Rector and inhabitants of the City of New York in Communion of the Church of England as by Law Established, for the encouraging and promoting the same good design, have sett apart a parcel of ground for that purpose, of upwards of Three Thousand Pounds value, belonging to the said Corporation, on the west side of the broadway, in the west ward of our City of New York, fronting easterly to Church street, between Barclay street and Murray street, four hundred and forty foot; And from thence runing westerly, between and along the said Barclay street and Murray street, to the North River; *And also*, a street, from the middle of the said Land, Easterly to the Broadway, of ninety Foot, to be called Robinson street. And have declared that they are ready and desirous to Convey the said Land in Fee, to and for the use of a College, intended and proposed to be Erected and Established in our said Province, upon the terms in their said declaration mentioned:

And Whereas our Loving Subjects, the Trustees, appointed in and by an act of the Governor, Council, and General Assembly of our said Province of New York, Intitled an Act for Vesting in Trustees the sum of three Thousand four Hundred and forty three Pounds eighteen shillings, by way of Lottery, for erecting a College within this Colony, esteeming the said Lands offered and sett apart by the said Rector and Inhabitants of the City of

10

New York, in Communion of the Church of England, as by Law Established, the most convenient place for the Building, Erecting, and Establishing, a College, in our said Province, have, by their humble petition, presented to our trusty and well Beloved *James De Lancey, Esq.*, our Lieutenant Governor and Commander in Chief of our said Province of New York, *In Council*, prayed our Letters patent of Incorporation for the Better Establishing, Erecting, and Building a College, on the said Lands, and the more Effectually Governing, Carrying on, and Promoting the same, and Instructing of Youth in the Liberal Arts and Sciences:

Wherefore Wee, being willing to Grant the Reasonable request and desire of our said Loving Subjects, and to Encourage the said good design of promoting a Liberal Education among them, and to make the same as Beneficial as may be, not only to the Inhabitants of our said Province of New York, But to all our Colonies and Territories in America.

Know De, that Wee, considering the premises, do of our especial Grace, Certain Knowledge, and meer motion, by these presents, will, Grant, Constitute, and ordain, that when and as soon as the said Rector and Inhabitants of the City of New York in Communion of the Church of England as by Law established, shall legally convey and assure the said herein before mentioned Lands to the Corporation, or body politick, Erected and made by these our Letters patent, That there be erected and made on the said Lands, a College, and other Buildings and Improvements, for the use and conveniency of the same, which shall be called and Known by the name of *Kings College*, for the Instruction and Education of Youth in the Learned Languages, and Liberal Arts and Sciences; *And* that in Consideration of such Grant, to be made by the Rector and Inhabitants of the City of New York, in Communion of the Church of England, as by Law Established, the President of the said College, for the time being, shall for ever hereafter be a member of, and in Communion with the Church of England, as by Law established; And that the Governors of the said College, and their successors, for ever, shall be one body Corporate and politick, in deed, fact, and name, and shall be called, named, and distinguished, by the name of the Governors of the

College of the Province of New York, in the City of New York, in America, and them and their successors, by the name of the Governors of the College of the Province of New York, in the City of New York, in America, one Body Corporate and politick, in deed, fact, and name, really and fully, we do for us, our heirs and Successors, Erect, Ordain, make, Constitute, declare, and Create by these presents, and that by that name, they shall and may have perpetual succession:

𝕬𝖓𝖉 𝖜𝖊 𝖉𝖔 for us, our heirs, and successors, for the Continuance and Better Establishment of the said College, Will, Give, Grant, Ordain, Constitute, and appoint, that in the said College, to be Erected and Built upon the Lands aforesaid, there shall from henceforth forever be a Body Corporate and politick, Consisting of the Governors of the College of the Province of New York, in the City of New York, in America; And for the more full and perfect Erection of the said Corporation and Body politick, consisting of the Governors of the College of the Province of New York, in the City of New York in America, we do will, Grant, ordain, Constitute, assign, Limitt, and appoint, by these presents, the most Reverend Father in God, our Trusty, and well beloved Thomas, Lord Archbishop of Canterbury, and the most Reverend the Lord Archbishop of Canterbury for the time being; The Right Honorable Dunk, Earl of Halifax, first Lord Commissioner for Trade and Plantations, and the first Lord Commissioner for Trade and plantations for the time being; Our now Lieutenant Governor and Commander in chief of our said Province of New York, and the Governor or Commander in chief of our said Province for the time being; the eldest Councilor of our said Province now and for the time being; the Judges of our Supreme Court of Judicature of our said Province now and for the time being; the Secretary of our said Province now and for the time being; the Attorney General of our said Province now and for the time being; the Speaker of the General Assembly of our said Province now and for the time being; the Treasurer of our said Province now and for the time being; the Mayor of our City of New York in our said Province now and for the time being; the Rector of Trinity Church in our said City of New York now and for the time being; the Senior Minister of the Re-

formed Protestant Dutch Church in our said City now and for
the time being; the Minister of the ancient Lutheran Church in
our said City now and for the time being; the Minister of the
French Church in our said City now and for the time being; the
Minister of the Presbeterian Congregation in our said City for
the time being; the President of the said College, appointed by
these Presents, and the President of the said College for the
time being, to be chosen as herein after is directed, and twenty
four other Persons, Who shall be called and named, and are
hereby called and named, the Governors of the College of the
Province of New York, in the City of New York, in America;

𝕬𝖓𝖉 𝖋𝖔𝖗 𝖙𝖍𝖆𝖙 purpose, We have elected, nominated, ordained,
constituted, limited, and appointed, and by these Presents do,
for us, our Heirs, and Successors, elect, nominate, ordain, con-
stitute, limit, and appoint, the said most Reverend Father in
God, Thomas, Lord Archbishop of Canterbury, and the Lord
Archbishop of Canterbury for the time being; The Right Hon-
ourable Dunk, Earl of Halifax, first Lord Commissioner for
Trade and Plantations, and the first Lord Commissioner for
Trade and Plantations for the time being; our now Lieutenant
Governor and Commander in Chief of our Province of New
York, and the Governor or Commander in chief of our said
Province for the time being; the eldest Councilor of our said
Province now and for the time being; the Judges of our Supreme
Court of Judicature of our said Province now and for the time
being; the Secretary of our said Province now and for the time
being; the Attorney General of our said Province now and for
the time being; the Speaker of the General Assembly of our
said Province now and for the time being; the Treasurer of our
said Province now and for the time being; the Mayor of our
said City of New York now and for the time being; the Rector
of Trinity Church in our said City now and for the time being;
the Senior Minister of the Reformed Protestant Dutch Church
in our said City now and for the time being; the Minister of
the ancient Lutheran Church in our said City now and for the
time being; the minister of the French Church in our said City
now and for the time being; the minister of the Presbeterian
Congregation in our said City for the time being; the President
of the said College, appointed by these Presents, and the Pres-

ident of the said College for the time being; and Archibald Kennedy, Joseph Murray, Josiah Martin, Paul Richard, Henry Cruger, William Walton, John Watts, Henry Beekman, Philip Ver Planck, Frederick Philipse, Joseph Robinson, John Cruger, Oliver De Lancey, James Livingston, Esquires, Benjamin Nicoll, William Livingston, Joseph Read, Nathaniel Marston, Joseph Haynes, John Livingston, Abraham Lodge, David Clarkson, Leonard Lispenard, and James De Lancey the Younger, Gentlemen, to be the present Governors of the said College; and we do by these Presents ordain and appoint our well beloved Samuel Johnson, Doctor of Divinity, to be the first and present President of the said College, for and during his Good Behaviour; and do will that he and the President for the time being after him, who shall also hold his office during Good behaviour, shall have the Immediate care of the Education and Government of the students that shall be sent to and admitted into the said College for Instruction and Education, according to such Rules and orders as shall be made by the Governors of the said College; *And* they are by these presents made and constituted a Body Corporate and politick, by the said name of the Governors of the College of the province of New York, in the City of New York, in America; and they and their successors, by the said name of the Governors of the College of the province of New York, in the City of New York, in America, be, and for ever hereafter shall be, a Body politick and Corporate, in deed, fact, and name, and shall be Capable and able in Law to sue and be sued, Implead and be Impleaded, answer and be Answered unto, Defend and be Defended, In all Courts and places, before Us, our Heirs and Successors, and before all and any the Judges, Justices, Officers, and Ministers of Us, our Heirs and Successors, in any Court or Courts, place and places Whatsoever, in all and all manner of actions, suits, Complaints, Pleas, causes, matters, and demands whatsoever, and of what kind or nature soever, in as full, ample manner and form as any of our other Liege Subjects of our said Province of New York can or may sue and be sued, Implead and be Impleaded, defend and be Defended, by any Lawfull ways and means whatsoever.

And, also, that they and their successors, by the said name of the Governors of the College of the Province of New York, in the City of New York, in America, be, and for ever hereafter, shall be a Body Corporate, Capable and able in Law to purchase, take, hold, receive, Enjoy, and have any messuages, houses, Lands, Tenements, and Hereditaments, and real Estate whatsoever, in Fee simple, or for Term of Life, or Lives, or Years, or in any other manner howsoever, for the use of the said College; *Provided always*, the clear yearly value thereof do not exceed the sum of Two Thousand pounds Stirling; and also Goods, Chattells, Books, moneys, annuities, and all other things of what nature and kind soever. *And, also,* that they and their Successors, by the same name of the Governours of the College of the Province of New York, in the City of New York, in America, to and for the use of the said College, shall and may have full power and authority to Erect and build any house or houses, or other Buildings, as they shall think necessary or convenient; and also to Give, Grant, Bargain, sell, demise, assign, or otherwise dispose of all or any messuages, Lands, Tenements, Rents, and other Hereditaments, and real Estate, and all Goods, Chattells, money, and other things whatsover, as to them shall seem fitt, either in the payment of the Salary or Salaries of the President, Fellows, and Professors of the said College, or any other officers or ministers of the same, at their will and pleasure; excepting always, and it is, *Nevertheless*, our True Intent and meaning that the said Governors of the said College for the time being, and their Successors, or any of them, shall not do or suffer to be done, at any time hereafter, any act or thing whereby or by means whereof the Lands set apart and offered to be Conveyed by the Rector and Inhabitants of the City of New York, In Communion of the Church of England as by Law Established, for the use of the College, or any part thereof, shall be Vested, Conveyed, or Transferred, to any other person, contrary to the true meaning hereof, other than by such Leases as are hereafter mentioned: our will and pleasure is, therefore, and we do for us our heirs and Successors will and ordain, that no Grant or Lease of the said Land, or any part thereof, shall be made by the said Governors of the said College which shall exceed the number of Twenty one Years, and That either in possession or not above three years before the End and

Expiration or Determination of the Estate or Estates in possession.

𝔄𝔫𝔡 𝔴𝔢 𝔡𝔬 by these presents will, ordain and direct, that the
said Governors of the said College (Except always the Lord
Archbishop of Canterbury for the time being, and our first Lord
Commissioner for Trade and Plantations) do, at their first meeting, after the receipt of these our Letters patents, and before
they proceed to any business of and concerning the said College,
take the oaths appointed to be taken by an act passed in the
first year of our Late Royal Father's Reign, Entituled, [an Act
for the further security of his Majesty's Person and Government,
and the Succession of the Crown, in the Heirs of the late Prin-
cess Sophia, being protestants, and for extinguishing the Hopes
of the pretended Prince of wales, and his open and Secret abet-
tors,] and make and subscribe the declaration mentioned in An
Act of Parliament made in the twenty fifth year of the Reign of
King Charles the second, Entituled, [an act for preventing Dan-
gers which may happen from popish Recusants;] *as also,* an
oath, faithfully to execute the trust Reposed in them, as members of the said Corporation, which Oaths we authorize and
Impower the Justices of our Supreme Court of Judicature, for
our said Province of New York for the time being, any or either
of them to administer; and that when, and as often as any person or persons, either by his office or place in our said Government, or Elsewhere, (Except always the Lord Archbishop of
Canterbury for the time being, and our first Lord Commissioner for Trade and Plantations for the time being,) or by
Choice of the said Governors of the said College, shall become,
or be Chosen a Member or members of the said Corporation,
they shall, before they are admitted, or enter into the said office
or Trust, take the said Oaths, and subscribe the said Declaration
to be administered to them in the manner above directed.

𝔄𝔫𝔡 𝔴𝔢 𝔡𝔬 further will, ordain, and direct, that the Governors
of the said College shall yearly, and every year hereafter, forever, on the Second Tuesday in the Month of May, in every
year, meet together in our said City of New York, for the Better taking care of, and Promoting the Interest of the said College; and that the said Governors of the said College, or any
fifteen or more of them being met, shall be a Legal meeting of

the said Corporation, and they, or the major part of them so met, shall have full power and authority to adjourn from day to day, as the Business of the said College may require, and to do, execute, and perform, all and every act and acts, thing and things whatsoever, which the said Governors of the said College are, or shall by these, our Letters patent, be authorized and Impowered to do, act, or Transact, in as full and ample manner, as if all and every of the members of the said Corporation were present.

And we do will, ordain, and direct, that as our Right Trusty and well beloved Thomas, Lord Archbishop of Canterbury, and the Lord Archbishop of Canterbury for the time being; and our said first Lord Commissioner for Trade and Plantations, and the First Lord Commissioner for Trade and plantations for the time being, cannot attend the meetings of the said Corporation, they and each of them shall, from time to time, have full power and authority to appoint a Proxy, in writing, under their hand and seal, which person or persons so appointed by them, and each of them shall and may Represent them, and each of them, Respectively, according to such appointment, and shall have full power to vote and act as a Governor or Governors of the said Corporation, at any and every meeting of the said Corporation, as fully and amply as if they, the Constituents, and each of them were present at every such meeting or meetings; *And*, *in Case* any other meeting or meetings of the said Governors of the said College shall, at any other time or times, be Judged and deemed Necessary for the Carrying on and promoting of the Business and Interest of the said College, or the Government thereof, by any five members of the said Corporation, we do, by these presents, authorize and Impower such five members, by writing, under their hands, to direct the Clerk of the said Corporation to Give notice of the day appointed by them, for such meeting, at the said City of New York, by advertising the same in one or more of the public news papers, at Least, seven Days before such meeting; and, that at such meeting, the said Clerk, before entering on any Business, shall Certify such Notification, under his hand, to the Board then met; *Provided, always,* Fifteen or more of the said members shall be then met together, which said fifteen or more members, so met, *In pursuance* of such Notification, shall be a Legal meeting of the said Governors of the said College; and they, or the major part of them so mett, shall have full power and authority to adjourn from day to day, as the Business of the said College may require, and to do, Transact, and perform, all matters and things whatsoever, that the said Governors of the said College are, or shall be authorized and Impowered to do, by these presents.

And, of our further Grace, Certain Knowledge, and meer motion, to the Intent that the said Corporation and Body politick, may answer the end of their erection and Constitution, and may have perpetual succession and Continue forever, Wee do for us, our heirs and Successors, Give and Grant unto the said Governors of the said College of the Province of New York, in the City of New York in America, and to their Successors for ever, that when and as often as they or any fifteen or more of the said members of the said Corporation or of their Successors shall be mett together at their said Yearly meeting herein before appointed, or at any other meeting upon Notification, as aforesaid, for the Service of the said College, that the Governor or Commander in chief of our said Province of New York, and, in his absence, the First person in Rank in our said Government, who holds his place as a Governor of the said Corporation by his office, place, or Dignity, and, in the absence of such, the Eldest Governor or member of the said Corporation then present, such Seniority to be taken according as they are named in this our Charter, during the lives of the present Governors, and after their death, the Seniority to be taken and accounted as they have been a Longer or shorter time Governors of the said Corporation, shall preside at such meeting from time to time, and that at such meeting or meetings from time to time, they or the major part of them so met, shall have full power and authority to Elect, nominate, and appoint any person to be president of the said College in a Vacancy of the said Presidentship for and during his Good Behaviour; provided, always, such President Elect or to be elected by them, be a member of, and in Communion with the Church of England, as by Law Established; and, also, to Elect one or more Fellow or Fellows, Professor or Professors, Tutor or Tutors, to assist the President of the said College in the Education and Government of the Students belonging to the said College, which Fellow or Fellows, Professor or Professors, Tutor or Tutors, and every of them, shall hold and Enjoy their said office or place, either at the will and pleasure of the Governors of the said Corporation, or during his or their Good Behaviour, according as shall be agreed upon Between such Fellow or Fellows, Professor or Professors, Tutor or Tutors, and the said Governors of the said College, *Provided, always*, such Fellow or Fellows, Professor or Professors, Tutor or Tutors, before they or either of them enter into or take upon themselves such office, do take the Oaths and subscribe the declaration hereinbefore directed, to be Taken and subscribed by the Governors of the said College before they enter upon their said Respective offices; and that when and as often as any or either of the said offices shall become Vacant by death or otherwise, the said Governors or the major part of any Fifteen or more of them so met as aforesaid, shall have full power to Elect, Nominate, and appoint, other or others in their places, upon the same proviso or Condition as aforesaid; and, *Also*, to Elect, Nominate, and appoint, upon the Death, Removal, Refusal to Qualify, or other vacancy of the place or places, of any Governor or Governors of the said Corporation not holding his office or place as a member of the same, by virtue of any other station, office, place, or dignity, from time to time, other or others in their places or stead as often as such vacancy shall happen, which Governor or Governors so from time to time elected and appointed, shall, by virtue of these presents, and of such Election and appointment be vested with all the powers, authoritys, and priviledges, which any Governor of the said Corporation is hereby Invested with.

And, we do further, of our especial Grace, certain Knowledge, and meer motion, for us, our heirs, and Successors, Grant and ordain that when and as often as the president of the said College, or any Fellow, Professor or Tutor holding his place during Good behaviour shall misdemean himself in his or their said offices, and thereupon a Complaint or Charge in writing of such misdemeanour shall be exhibited against him or them by any member of the said Corporation, at any meeting or meetings of the said Corporation met and convened as aforesaid, That it shall be Lawful for the said members of the said Corporation

then met, or the major part of them from time to time, upon
Examination and due proof, to suspend or discharge such
President, Fellow, Professor, or Tutor, from his said office, and
other or others in his or their place or places to appoint; and
we do further for us, our heirs, and Successors, will and Grant
that the said Governors of the said College, or the major part
of any fifteen or more of them Convened and mett as aforesaid,
shall and may, from time to time, as occasion may require,
Elect, Constitute, and appoint, a Treasurer, Clerk, and Steward,
for the said College, and to appoint them and each of them
their respective Business and Trusts, and to displace and discharge from the Service of the said College such Treasurer,
Clerk, or steward, and to elect other or others in their places
and stead; and such Treasurer, Clerk, and steward, so Elected
and appointed, we do for us, our heirs, and Successors, by these
presents Constitute and Establish in their several offices, and do
Give them full power and authority to Exercise the same in the
said College, according to the direction and during the pleasure
of the said Governors of the said College, or the major part of
any fifteen or more of them Convened as aforesaid, as fully and
freely as any other the like officers in any of our universities or
any of our Colleges in that part of our Kingdom of Great
Britain called England, Lawfully may and ought to do: and we
do further, of our Especial Grace, Certain Knowledge, and meer
motion, Give and Grant unto the said Governors of the said
College, that they and their Successors, or the major part of any
fifteen or more of them Convened and mett Together in manner
aforesaid, shall and may direct and appoint what Books shall
be publickly read and taught in the said College, by the President, Fellows, Professors, and Tutors; and shall and may, under
their Common seal, make and set down, and they are hereby
fully Impowered, from time to time, to make and set down in
writing, such Laws, ordinances, and orders, for the Better
Government of the said College, and Students, and Ministers
thereof, as they shall think best for the General Good of the
same, so that they are not Repugnant to the Laws and statutes
of that part of our Kingdom of Great Britain called England,
or of our said Province of New York, and do not extend to
exclude any person of any Religious Denomination whatever

from Equal Liberty and advantage of Education, or from any of the Degrees, Liberties, Priviledges, Benefits, or Immunities of the said College, on account of his particular Tenets in matters of Religion; *And* such laws, Ordinances, and orders, which shall be so made as aforesaid, we do by these Presents, for us, our heirs, and Successors, Ratify, Confirm, and allow, as Good and Effectual to bind and oblige all and every the Students and Officers and Ministers of the said College; and we do hereby authorize and Impower the said Governors of the said College, or the major part of any fifteen or more of them, at any of their meetings Convened as aforesaid, and the President, Fellows, and Professors for the time being, to put such Laws, ordinances, and orders, in execution, that is to say, such as Inflict upon any Student the Greater Punishments of Expulsion, Suspension, Degradation, and public Confession, by the Governors of the said College, or the major part of any fifteen or more of them, convened and met Together as aforesaid only; and such as Inflict the Lesser Punishments, by the President, Fellows, and Professors, or any of them, according to the true Intent of such Laws, ordinances, and orders, as shall be made In Pursuance of these presents for that purpose.

And we do further will, ordain, and direct, that there shall be forever hereafter Publick morning and evening service Constantly performed in the said College, morning and evening for ever, by the President, Fellows, Professors, or Tutors, of the said College, or one of them, according to the Liturgy of the Church of England as by Law Established, or such a Collection of prayers out of the said Liturgy, with a Collect peculiar for the said College, as shall be approved of from time to time by the Governors of the said College, or the major part of any fifteen or more of them Convened as aforesaid: and we do further will and Grant, that the said Governors of the said College for the time being, or the major part of any fifteen or more of them Convened as aforesaid, shall have full power and Lawful authority to visit, order, punish, place, and displace, The Treasurer, Clerk, Steward, students, and other officers and ministers of the said College, and to order, Reform, and Redress, all and any the disorders, misdemeanors and abuses in the persons aforesaid, or any of them, and to Censure, suspend or deprive them, or any or either of them, *So always*, that no visitation, act, or thing, in or Concerning the said College, be made or done by any other person or persons whatsoever but as is herein before Directed and Declared.

And we do further, of our Especial Grace, Certain Knowledge, and meer motion, will, Give, and Grant, unto the said Governors of the said College, that for the Encouragement of the Students of the said College to Diligence and Industry in their Studies, that they and their Successors, and the major part of any fifteen or more of them Convened and mett together as aforesaid, do, by the President of the said College, or any other person or persons by them authorized and appointed, Give and Grant any such degree and degrees to any the students of the said College, or any other person or persons by them thought worthy thereof, as are usually Granted by any or either of our universities or Colleges in that part of our Kingdom of Great Britain called England, and that the President, or such other persons to be appointed for that purpose as aforesaid, do sign and seal Diplomas or Certificates of such Degree or Degrees, to be kept by the Graduates as a Testimonial thereof.

And further, *of* our Especial Grace, Certain Knowledge, and meer motion, we do for us, our heirs, and Successors, will, Give, and Grant, unto the said Governors of the said College, and to their Successors, that they shall and may have one Common Seal, under which they shall and may pass all Grants, Diplomas, and all other writings whatsoever, requisite, necessary, or Convenient to pass under the seal of the said Corporation; which seal shall be Engraven in such form and with such Devices and Inscriptions as shall be agreed upon by the said Governors of the said College, or the major part of any fifteen or more of them that shall be Convened for the service of the said College, in the manner above directed; and by these our Letters patent it shall and may be Lawful for them and their Successors, at any of their meetings Convened as aforesaid, as they shall see cause, to Break, Change, alter, and new make the same, or any other common Seal, when and as often as to them shall seem convenient.

And we, further, for us, our heirs, and Successors, Give and Grant unto the said Governors of the said College, and their

Successors, or the major part of any fifteen or more of them Convened as aforesaid, full power and authority, from time to time, and at all times hereafter, to nominate and appoint all other Inferior officers or Ministers which they shall think convenient and necessary for the use of the College, not herein particularly named or mentioned, which Officers and Ministers we do hereby Impower to execute their Respective offices or Trusts, during the will and pleasure only of the Governors of the said College, or the major part of any fifteen or more of them Convened as aforesaid, as fully and freely as any other the like Officers or ministers in and of our Universities or any other College in that part of our Kingdom of Great Britain Called England may or ought to do.

And, Lastly, of our Express will and pleasure, and meer motion, we do, for us, our heirs, and Successors, Give and Grant unto the said Governors of the said College, and to their Successors for ever, that these our Letters patent, being entered of Record, as is herein after particularly Expressed, or the Enrollment thereof, shall be Good and Effectual in the Law, to all Intents and purposes, against us, our heirs, and Successors, without any other Lycense, Grant, or Confirmation, from *us*, our heirs, or Successors, hereafter by the said Governors of the said College to be had or obtained, Notwithstanding the not reciting or misrecital, or not naming or misnaming, of the aforesaid offices, Franchises, Priviledges, Immunities, or other the premisses, or any of them; and notwithstanding a writt *ad Quod Damnum* hath not issued forth to inquire of or concerning the Premisses, or any of them, before the ensealing hereof, any Statute, act, Ordinance, or provision, or any other matter or thing to the Contrary thereof in any wise Notwithstanding; *To have, hold, and Enjoy*, all and singular the Priviledges, Liberties, advantages, and Immunities, and all and singular other the Premisses herein or hereby Granted, or meant, mentioned, or Intended to be herein and hereby Given and Granted unto them, the said Governors of the said College of the Province of New York, in the City of New York, in America, and to their Successors for ever.

In Testimony whereof, we have caused these our Letters to be made patent, and the Great seal of our Province of New

York to be hereunto affixed, and the same to be entered of Record in our Secretary's office of our said Province, in one of the Books of Patents there Remaining.

𝔚𝔦𝔱𝔫𝔢𝔰𝔰 our Trusty and well beloved *James De Lancey, Esq.*, our Lieutenant Governor, and Commander in chief in and over our Province of New York, and the Territories depending thereon, in *America*, in, by, and with the Advice and Consent of our Council of our said Province, this thirty first day of October, in the year of our Lord one thousand seven hundred and fifty four, and of our Reign the twenty eighth. The following Erasures and Interlineations appearing in these our Letters Patent. That is to say, in the first skin, Line four, the word [Law]. Line nineteen, these words, [by these our Letters Patent, that there be Erected and made] Interlined: line twenty one, [with] wrote on Eraisure: line twenty two, [Law] Interlined. In the second skin, line Twelve, [the] interlined, and [Younger] wrote on Eraisure. In the third skin, the First line, [and secret,] and in the sixth Line, [Administered] wrote partly on eraisure. In the twelfth line, [And the first Lord Commissioner for Trade and Plantations] Interlined. And in the fourth skin, and first line, the word [*And*] Interlined.

CLARKE, Junior.

[GREAT SEAL OF THE PROVINCE.]

PETITION FOR ADDITIONAL CHARTER.

To the Honourable James De Lancey Esqr., his Majesty's Lieut. Governour and Commander in Chief of the Province of New York and Territories thereon depending, in Councill.

The Petition of the Governours of the College of the Province of New York in the City of New York in America.

Humbly sheweth.

That Whereas by his Majesty's Letters Patent of Incorporation bearing date the 31st of October 1754, the sole power of electing Professors in said College is vested in said Governours, and

Whereas Your Honour's Petitioners humbly conceive, that it will tend to the Prosperity of the College, and the increase of the number of Students if Provision could be made, for establishing a Professorship in Divinity, for the Instruction of such Youth, as may intend to devote themselves to the sacred Ministry in those Churches, in this Province, that are in Communion with and conform to the Doctrine discipline and Worship established in the united Provinces by the National Synod of Dort, and any other students that may be desirous to attend his Lectures.

Your Honour's Petitioners therefore humbly pray, that an Additional Charter be Granted them for that Purpose, and that the nomination of such Professor from time to time be in the Minister Elders and Deacons of the Reformed Protestant Dutch Church in this City and the same established in such manner as shall seem best to your Honour. And Your Petitioners as in duty bound shall ever pray.

Wm. Kempe,	Philip Ver Planck,
A. D: Peyster,	Fred. Philipse,
Hen. Barclay,	Jos. Robinson,
Joannes Ritzema,	John Cruger,
John Albert Weygand,	James Livingston,
Joannes Carle,	B. Nicoll,
Samuel Johnson,	Jos. Reade,
Josiah Martin,	Nathal. Marston,
Paul Richard,	Joseph Haynes,
Hen. Cruger,	Jno. Livingston,
Jno. Watts,	David Clarkson,
Henry Beekman,	Leonard Lispenard,

James De Lancey.

New York, May 13th, 1755.

ADDITIONAL CHARTER OF The Governors of the College of the Province of New-York in the City of New-York in America.

George the Second, by the Grace of God, of Great-Britain, France and Ireland, King, Defender of the Faith and so forth, TO ALL to whom these presents shall come, Greeting.

Whereas Our loving Subjects, The Governors of the College of the Province of New-York, in the City of New-York, in America, by their humble Petition presented to Our Trusty and Well-beloved JAMES DE LANCEY, Esq; Our Lieutenant Governor and Commander in Chief of Our said Province of New-York, IN COUNCIL, have set forth, That although by Our Letters Patent of Incorporation, bearing Date the Thirty First Day of October last past, the sole Power of electing Professors in said College, is vested in the said Governors: Yet the said Petitioners humbly conceived, that it would tend to the Prosperity of the College, and the Increase of the Number of Students, if Provision could be made for establishing a Professorship in Divinity in the same, for the Instruction of such Youth as may intend to devote themselves to the sacred Ministry, in those Churches in this Province that are in Communion with, and conform to the Doctrine, Discipline and Worship established in the United Provinces, by the National Synod of Dort; and any other Students that may be desirous to attend his Lectures: And therein did humbly pray, That an additional CHARTER might be granted them for that Purpose; and that the Nomination of such Professor, from Time to Time, be in the Minister, Elders and Deacons of the Reformed Protestant Dutch Church in the City of New-York.

And whereas upon the Surrender of this Our Province by the Dutch, in the Year of Our Lord One Thousand Six Hundred and Sixty-four, it is provided by the Eighth Article of Surrender, That the Dutch here shall enjoy the Liberty of their Consciences in Divine Worship and Church Discipline. And We being willing and desirous, that all Our Loving Subjects, the Members of the Reformed Protestant Dutch Churches, who are very numerous

in Our Government of New-York, should always continue as
they have hitherto done, to enjoy the Liberty of their Consciences in Divine Worship and Church Discipline, and that
they may always have learned Pastors and Teachers to instruct
and assist them therein; as also to promote the Prosperity of
the aforesaid College, and the Increase of the Number of
Students therein. KNOW YE, That of Our especial Grace, certain Knowledge, and meer Motion, We have willed, granted,
constituted and appointed, and by these Presents, Do will and
grant to the Governors of the College of the Province of New-
York, in the City of New-York in America, and to their Successors, that from Time to Time, and at all Times hereafter
FOREVER, there may, and shall be in the said College, a Professor of Divinity of the Reformed Protestant Dutch Church,
for the Instruction of such Youth as may intend to devote themselves to the sacred Ministry in those Churches, in this Our
Province of New-York, that are in Communion with, and conform to the Doctrine, Discipline and Worship established in the
United Provinces, by the National Synod of Dort; and any
other Students that may be desirous to attend his Lectures.

And We do, by these Presents, will, give, grant and appoint,
That such Professor shall be from Time to Time, and at all
Times hereafter, nominated, chosen and appointed by the
Ministers, Elders and Deacons of the Reformed Protestant
Dutch Church, in the City of New-York, for the Time being,
when they shall see fit to make such Nomination, Choice and
Appointment. And they are hereby fully impowered and author-
ized to make such Nomination, Choice and Appointment; and
are hereby required to certify such Nomination, Choice and
Appointment, to the Governors of the said College, under their
Corporation Seal: Provided always, such Professor so to be
chosen from Time to Time by them, be a Member of, and in
Communion with the said Reformed Protestant Dutch Church.
And thereupon the Governors of the said College, and the
President thereof for the Time being, shall, and are hereby
required and commanded to receive and admit him accordingly:
Any Thing in Our herein before-mentioned Charter of Incor-
poration to the contrary hereof in any wise notwithstanding.
Which Professor of Divinity, We will and direct, shall, before

he enter into or take upon himself such Office, take the Oaths
and subscribe the Declaration directed in Our CHARTER aforesaid, for the other Professors and Officers of the said College to
take, before one of the Judges of Our Supreme Court of Judicature for Our said Province of New-York, who is hereby impowered and authorized to administer the same.

And We do further will, ordain and grant, That the said Professor of Divinity, shall hold his said Place or Office during his
good Behaviour, or during Will and Pleasure, according to
such Agreement as shall be made between him and the said
Minister, Elders and Deacons of the Reformed Protestant Dutch
Church, at the Time of his Nomination and Appointment; and
be intituled unto, and have, exercise and enjoy the same, and
like Powers, Privileges, and Authorities in the said College, as
other Professors of and in the same do or may have, hold, exercise, or enjoy in the same.   And also shall demean and conform
himself to such Rules, Laws and Regulations as the other Professors in the said College are or shall be obliged to conform
unto, and regulate themselves by.   And in Case he shall misdemean himself in his said Office, he shall be liable to be suspended or discharged from the same, in the same Manner as
other Professors of and in the said College are or may be suspended or discharged, by Virtue of Our aforesaid Charter of
Incorporation.

> **In testimony** whereof, We have caused these Our Letters
> to be made Patent, and the Great Seal of Our said
> Province to be hereunto affixed, and the same to be
> entered of Record in Our Secretary's Office, in Our
> City of New-York, in one of the Books of Patents
> there remaining.
>
> **Witness** Our said Trusty and Well-beloved JAMES
> DE LANCEY, Esq ; Our Lieutenant Governor and
> Commander in Chief, in and over Our Province of
> NEW-YORK, and Territories thereon depending in
> America; at Our Fort in Our City of NEW-YORK in
> and by the Advice and Consent of Our Council of
> Our said Province the Thirtieth Day of May, in the
> Year of Our Lord One Thousand Seven Hundred
> and Fifty Five, and of Our Reign the Twenty
> Eighth.
>
> CLARKE, junior.

[GREAT SEAL OF THE PROVINCE.]

ACTS RELATING TO THE COLLEGE.

An Act for appropriating the monies raised by diverse Lotteries for erecting or founding a College in this Colony.   Passed December 1, 1756.
                    Laws of 1756, Chap. 116.

Provides for the payment of one moiety or half part of the moneys raised by the Lotteries held under the preceding acts to the Governors of the College of the Province of New York, and the other moiety or half part to the Mayor, Aldermen and Commonalty of the City of New York, and provides for the payment to the Governors of £500 per annum for seven years. Under this act the College received £3,282.

CHARTER OF 1784.

An Act for granting certain privileges to the college heretofore called Kings College, for altering the name and charter thereof, and erecting an university within this State.   Passed May 1, 1784.
                    Laws of 1784, Chap. 51.

Whereas by letters patent under the great seal of the late colony of New York, bearing date the thirty-first day of October, in the twenty-eighth year of the reign of George the second the king of Great Britain, a certain body politic and corporate, was created by the name of the Governors of the College of the Province of New York in the city of New York in America, with divers privileges, capacities and immunities, as in and by the said patent will more fully appear.

And whereas there are many vacancies in the said corporation, occasioned by the death or absence of a great number of the governors of the said college, whereby the succession is so greatly broke in upon as to require the interposition of the Legislature.

And whereas the remaining governors of the said college, desireous to render the same extensively useful, have prayed, that the said college may be erected into an university, and that such other alterations may be made in the charter or letters of incorporation above recited, as may render them more conformable to the liberal principles of the Constitution of this State.

Be it therefore enacted by the People of the State of New York represented in Senate and Assembly and it is hereby enacted by the authority of the same, That all the rights priviledges and immunities heretofore vested in the corporation, heretofore known by the name of the Governors of the College of the Province of New York, in the city of New York in America, so far as they relate to the capacity of holding, or disposing of property either real or personal, of suing or being sued, of making laws or ordinances for their own government, or that of their servants, pupils and others, under their care and subject to their direction, of appointing, displacing and paying stewards and other inferior servants, of making, holding and having a common seal, of altering and changing the same at pleasure, be and they hereby are vested in the regents of the university of the State of New York, who are hereby erected into a corporation or body corporate and politic, and enabled to hold possess and enjoy the above mentioned rights, franchises, priviledges and immunities, together with such others as are contained in this act, by the name and stile of the Regents of the University of the State of New York, of whom the Governor, the Lieutenant Governor, the President of the Senate for the time being, the Speaker of the Assembly, the mayor of the city of New York, and the mayor of the city of Albany, the Attorney General and the Secretary of the State respectively for the time being, be and they hereby are severally constituted perpetual regents, in virtue of their several and respective offices, places and stations, and together with other persons herein after named to the number of twenty-four, to wit, Henry Brockholst Livingston and Robert Harpur of the city of New York, Walter Livingston and Christopher Yates of the county of Albany, Anthony Hoffman and Cornelius Humfrey of the county of Dutchess, Lewis Morris and Philip Pell Junior of the county of Westchester, Henry

Wisner and John Haring of the county of Orange, Christopher Tappen and James Clinton of the county of Ulster, Christopher P. Yates and James Livingston of the county of Montgomery, Abraham Bancker and John C. Dongan of the county of Richmond, Mathew Clarkson and Rutger Van Brunt of the county of Kings, James Townsend and Thomas Lawrence of the county of Queens, Ezra L'Hommedieu and Caleb Smith of the county of Suffolk, and John Williams and John McCrea of the county of Washington, be and they hereby are appointed regents of the said University and it shall and may be lawful to and for the clergy of the respective religious denominations in this State, to meet at such time and place, as they shall deem proper after the passing of this act, and being so met shall by a majority of voices of those who shall so meet, chuse and appoint one of their body to be a regent in the said university and in case of death or resignation to chose and appoint another in the same manner and the regent so chosen and appointed shall have the like powers as any other regent appointed or to be appointed by virtue of this act.   And to the end that a succession of regents be perpetually kept up.

Be it further enacted by the authority aforesaid, That whenever and so often as one or more of the regents of the said university, not being such in virtue of his or their office, place or station, shall remove his or their place of residence from within this State, shall resign or die, that the place or places of such regent or regents, so removing, resigning or dying shall be filled up by the governor or person administering the government of the State for the time being, by and with the advice and consent of the council of appointment, so that such appointments be of persons resident in the counties respectively wherein the former regents did reside, other than where such vacancy may happen of a regent appointed by the clergy as aforesaid.

And be it further enacted by the authority aforesaid, That as soon as may be after the passing of this act, the regents of the said university, shall by plurality of voices, chuse a chancellor a vice chancellor a treasurer and a secretary, from among the said regents, the said chancellor or in his absence the vice chancellor to preside at all elections and other meetings to be held by the said regents, and to have the casting vote upon every division.

And for the well ordering and directing of the said corporation.

Be it further enacted by the authority aforesaid, That the regents
of the said university, or a majority of them shall be and hereby
are vested with full power and authority to ordain and make
ordinances and bye laws for the government of the several colleges, which may or shall compose the said university, and the
several presidents, professors, tutors, fellows, pupils and servants
thereof and for the management of such estate as they may and
shall be invested with; that they shall have full power and
authority to determine the salaries of the officers and servants
of the said college to remove from office any such president
professor tutor fellow or servant, as they conceive, after a full
hearing to have abused their trust, or to be incompetent thereto,
provided nevertheless, that no fine to be levied by virtue of the
said laws or ordinances, shall exceed the value of one bushel of
wheat for any one offence, and that no pupil or student shall be
suspended for a longer term than twenty days, or be rusticated
or expelled, but upon a fair and full hearing of the parties, by
the chancellor or vice chancellor of the said university, and at
least ten of the regents not being president or professors of the
college to which the person accused belongs, or under whose
immediate direction the same may be, and the said regents are
hereby further impowered and directed as soon as may be, to
elect a president and professors for the college heretofore called
Kings College, which president shall continue in place during
the pleasure of the regents of the university. And that from
and after the first election, the said president and all future
presidents shall be elected, from out of the professors of the
several colleges, that may or shall compose the said university,
and that no professor shall in any wise whatsoever be accounted
ineligible, for or by reason of an religious tenet or tenets, that
he may or shall profess, or be compelled by any bye law or
otherwise, to take any religious test-oath whatsoever. And to
the end that the intention of the donors and benefactors of the
said beforementioned college be not defeated.

Be it further enacted by the authority aforesaid, That all the estate
whether real or personal, which the said governor of the corporation of Kings College held by virtue of the said beforementioned

charter, be held and possessed by the said regents and applied solely to the use of the said college and that the said regents may and there hereby are empowered to receive and hold for the use of the said college, an estate of the annual value of three thousand five hundred pounds, in manner specified in the first above recited charter or letters patent of incorporation. And for the further promotion of learning and the extension of literature.

Be it further enacted by the authority aforesaid, That the said regents may hold, and possess estates, real and personal to the annual amount of forty thousand bushels of wheat, over and above all profits arising from room rent or tuition money, and that whenever any lands tenements or hereditaments, or other estate real or personal, shall be given, granted or conveyed to the regents of the university of the State without expressing any designation thereof, such estate shall be applied in such manner as to the said regents shall seem most advantageous to the said university provided always, that whenever any gift, grant, bequest, devise or conveyance shall express the particular use to which the same is to be applied if adequate thereto, it shall be so applied and not otherwise.

And be it further enacted by the authority aforesaid, That the said regents be and they hereby are impowered, to found schools and colleges in any such part of this State as may seem expedient to them, and to endow the same, vesting such colleges so endowed with full and ample powers to confer the degrees of batchelor of arts, and directing the manner in which such colleges are to be governed, always reserving to the chancellor and vice chancellor of the university, and a certain number of the regents, to be appointed by a majority of the said regents, a right to visit and examine into the state of literature in such college, and to report to the regents at large any deficiency in the laws of such college or neglect in the execution thereof, every such school or college being at all times to be deemed a part of the university, and as such, subject to the controul and direction of the said regents; and if it should so happen, that any person or persons, or any body politic or corporate, should at his or their expense found any college or school, and endow the same with an estate, real or personal of the yearly value of one thousand bushels of wheat,

that such school or college shall on the application of the founder
or founders or their heirs or successors, be considered as com-
posing a part of the said university, and the estate thereunto
annexed shall be and hereby is vested in the said regents, of the
university, to be applied according to the intention of the donor,
and that the said founder and founders, and their heirs, or if a
body corporate, their successors shall be and hereby are forever
hereafter entitled to send a representative for such college or
school, who together with the president (if the estate is applied
to the use of a college) shall be and they hereby are at all times
hereafter to be considered as regents of the said university, and
vested with the like powers and authorities in all things, as in
and by this act is given to the other regents of the said university and the said college or school shall in all things, not particularly restricted by the donor, conform to the general laws
and regulations of the said university, provided that nothing in
this act contained shall be construed to deprive any person or
persons of the right to erect such schools and colleges as to him
or them may deem proper, independent of the said university.

And be it further enacted by the authority aforesaid, That whenever
any religious body or society of men shall deem it proper to institute a professorship in the said university for the promotion
of their particular religious tenets, or for any other purpose not
inconsistent with religion, morality and the laws of this State,
and shall appropriate a fund for that purpose, not being less
than two hundred bushel of wheat per annum, that the regents
of the said university shall cause the same to be applied as the
donors shall direct, for the purposes above mentioned, the said
professors so to be appointed to be subject to the like rules, laws
and ordinances, as other the professors of the said university,
and entitled to the like immunities and priviledges.

And be it further enacted by the authority aforesaid, That the said
regents and their successors forever, shall and may have full
power and authority by the chancellor or vice chancellor of the
said university, or any other person or persons by them authorized or appointed, to give and grant to any of the students of
the said university, or to any person or persons thought worthy
thereof all such degrees as well in divinity, philosophy, civil and
municipal laws, as in every other art, science and faculty what-

soever as are or may be conferred by all or any of the universities in Europe, and that the chancellor or in his absence the vice chancellor of the said university for the time being, do sign and seal with the seal of the said corporation diplomas or certificates of such degrees having been given, other than the degree of batchelor of arts, which shall and may be granted by the president of the college in which the person taking the same shall have been graduated, and the diploma's shall be signed by the said president. That the persons to be elected fellows professors or tutors as aforesaid, be also regents of the said university, ex officiis and capable of voting in every case relative only to the respective colleges to which they shall belong, excepting in such cases wherein they shall respectively be personally concerned or interested.

And be it further enacted by the authority aforesaid, That the college within the city of New York heretofore called Kings College, be forever here after called and known by the name of Columbia College.

An Act to amend an act entitled "An act for granting certain privileges to the college, heretofore called Kings college: for altering the name and charter thereof, and erecting an university within this State" passed the 1st day of May, 1784.   Passed November 26, 1784. Laws of 1785, Chapter 15.

Recites that, "*Whereas*, it is represented to the legislature, that the dispersed residences of many of the regents of the university of this State, and the largeness of the quorum who are made capable of business, the interest and prosperity of the said university, have been greatly obstructed. And it is also represented, that certain doubts have arisen as to the construction of the act entitled 'An act for granting certain privileges to the college heretofore called Kings-college, for altering the name and charter thereof and erecting an university within this State,' passed the 1st day of May, 1784. For remedy whereof." The act provides: "That in addition to the regents appointed in and by the before mentioned act, the several persons herein after named, shall be and hereby respectively are constituted regents of the said university (that is to say): John Jay, Samuel Provost, John H. Livingston, John Rodgers, John Mason, John Ganoe, John Daniel Gros, Johann Ch. Kunze, Joseph Delaplain, Gershom Seixas, Alexander Hamilton, John Laurance, John Rutherford, Morgan Lewis, Leonard Lispenard, John Cochran, Charles McKnight, Thomas Jones, Malachi Treat and Nicholas Romain of New York, Peter W. Yates, Mathew Vischer, and Heenlock Woodruf of Albany, George I. L. Doll of Ulster, John Vanderbilt of Kings, Thomas Romain of Montgomery, Samuel Buel of Suffolk, Gilbert Livingston of Dutchess, Nathan Kerr of Orange, Ebenezer Lockwood of Westchester, John Lloyd Jun of Queens, Harmanus Garrison of Richmond & Ebenezer Russell of Washington. And that the said respective regents, hereby constituted, shall enjoy the same power and authority, as are granted to, and vested in the other regents appointed by the said act, as fully and effectually, as if they had been therein expressly named." The act also provides for meetings and quorums of the regents, and authorizes the treasurer of the State to advance the sum of £2552 to the treasurer of the university for the use of Columbia College.

CHARTER OF 1787.

AN ACT TO INSTITUTE AN UNIVERSITY WITHIN THIS STATE AND FOR OTHER PURPOSES THEREIN MENTIONED.

PASSED APRIL 13, 1787.

LAWS OF 1787, CHAPTER 82.

Recites that:—"*Whereas*, by two acts of the legislature of the State of New York, the one passed the first day of May, and the other twenty sixth day of November, one thousand seven hundred and eighty four, an university is instituted within this State, in the manner and with the powers therein specified. And whereas from the representation of the regents of the said university, it appears there are defects in the constitution of the said university which call for alterations and amendments. And whereas a number of acts on the same subject amending correcting and altering former ones, tend to render the same less intelligible and easily to be understood. Whereof to the end, that the constitution of the said university may be properly amended and appear entire in one law, it will be expedient, to delineate and establish the same in this, and repeal all former acts relative thereto." The act provides for the establishment of a university to be called and known by the name or style of " The Regents of the University of the State of New York," and creates the regents a corporation, with power to visit and inspect all the colleges, academies or schools which are or may be established in the State, to confer diplomas, and to grant charters. The act further repeals the acts passed May 1st and November 26th, 1784, and provides:

And be it further enacted by the authority aforesaid, That the charter heretofore granted to the governors of the college of the province of New-York, in the city of New-York, in America, dated the thirty-first day of October, in the year of our Lord one thousand seven hundred and fifty-four, shall be, and hereby is fully and absolutely ratified and confirmed, in all respects, except that the college thereby established, shall be henceforth called Columbia College: That the style of the said corporation shall be, The trustees of Columbia College, in the city of New-York; and that no persons shall be trustees of the same, in virtue of any offices, characters, or descriptions whatever; excepting also such clauses thereof as require the taking of oaths, and subscribing the declaration therein mentioned; and which render a person ineligible to the office of president of the college, on account of his religious tenets, and prescribe a form of public prayer to be used in the said college; and also excepting the clause thereof which provides, that the by-laws and ordinances to be made in pursuance thereof, should not be repugnant to the laws and statutes of that part of the kingdom of Great-Britain, called England; except also, that in all cases where fifteen governors are required to constitute a quorum for the despatch of business, thirteen trustees shall be sufficient. Provided always, That the by-laws and ordinances to be made by the trustees of the said Columbia college, shall not be contrary

to the constitution and laws of this state.   (Repealed by Laws
of 1810, Chapter 85.)

And be it further enacted by the authority aforesaid, That James
Duane, Samuel Provost, John H. Livingston, Richard Varick,
Alexander Hamilton, John Mason, James Wilson, John Gano,
Brockholst Livingston, Robert Harpur, John Daniel Gross,
Johan Christoff Kunze, Walter Livingston, Lewis A. Scott,
Joseph Delaplaine, Leonard Lispenard, Abraham Beach, John
Lawrance, John Rutherford, Morgan Lewis, John Cochran,
Gershom Seixas, Charles McKnight, Thomas Jones, Malachi
Treat, Samuel Bard, Nicholas Romein, Benjamin Kissam, and
Ebenezer Crossby, shall be, and they are hereby constituted and
declared to be the present trustees of Columbia college, in the
city of New-York, and that when by the death or resignation, or
removal of any of the said trustees, the number of those trustees
shall be reduced to twenty-four, then and from thenceforth the
said twenty-four trustees shall be, and they hereby are declared
and constituted trustees of the said Columbia college, in perpetual succession, according to the true intent and meaning of
the said charter; and all vacancies thereafter shall be supplied
in the manner thereby directed.   (Repealed by Laws of 1810,
Chapter 85.)

And be it further enacted by the authority aforesaid, That all and
singular the power, authority, rights, privileges, franchises, and
immunities, so heretofore granted to, and vested in the said
governors of the college of the province of New-York, in the
city of New-York, in America, by the said charter, excepting as
before excepted, shall be, and the same hereby are granted to
and vested in the trustees of Columbia college, in the city of
New-York, and their successors forever, as fully and effectually,
to all intents and purposes, as if the same were herein particularly specified and expressed; and all and singular the lands,
tenements, hereditaments, and real estate, goods, chattels, rents,
annuities, moneys, books, and other property, whereof the said
governors of the college of the province of New-York, in the
city of New-York, in America, were seised, possessed, or entitled,
under and in virtue of the said charter, or with which the
regents of the said university were invested, under or by virtue
of the said acts, for the use or benefit of the said Columbia col-

lege, shall be, and the same hereby are granted to and vested in the said trustees of Columbia college, in the city of New-York, and their successors forever, for the sole use and benefit of the said college; and it shall and may be lawful to and for the said trustees, and their successors, to grant, bargain, sell, demise, improve, and dispose of the same, as to them shall seem meet. Provided, always, That the lands given and granted to the governors of the college of the province of New-York, in the city of New-York, in America, by the corporation heretofore styled, The rector and inhabitants of the city of New-York, in communion of the church of England, as by law established, on part whereof the said college is erected, shall not be granted for any greater estate, or in any other manner, than is limited by the said charter. (Repealed by Laws of 1810, Chapter 85.)

And be it further enacted by the authority aforesaid, That when any special meeting of the trustees of the said college shall be deemed necessary, it shall and may be lawful to and for the senior trustee of the said college, then in the city of New-York, and taking upon himself the exercise of his office, (which seniority shall be determined according to the order in which the said trustees are named in this act, and shall be elected hereafter,) and he is hereby authorized and required, on application for that purpose in writing under the hands of any five or more of the said trustees, to appoint a time for such special meeting, in some convenient place within the said city, and to cause due notice thereof to be given in the manner directed by the said charter. (Repealed by Laws of 1810, Chapter 85.)

And be it further enacted by the authority aforesaid, That the act, entitled, An act for granting certain privileges to the college heretofore called King's college, for altering the name and charter thereof, and erecting a university within this state, passed the 1st day of May, 1784; and the act, entitled, An act to amend an act, entitled, An act for granting certain privileges to the college heretofore called King's college, for altering the name and charter thereof, and erecting an university within this state, passed the 26th day of November, 1784, be, and they are hereby severally repealed.

An Act to encourage Literature, by Donations to Columbia College, and to the several Academies in the State. Passed April 11, 1792.
Laws of 1792, Chapter 69.

Whereas it has been represented to the legislature, that the funds of Columbia college, in this state, have, in consequence of events which took place during the late war, been so far diminished, as to render it impracticable for the trustees to defray certain necessary expenses which have accrued to the college in consequence of the alterations in the streets of the city of New York, and to repair the losses which the college sustained during the late war, with respect to its library, and to incur such further expenses as would render the seminary more extensively useful, without pecuniary aid from the legislature: For remedy whereof,

Be it enacted by the People of the State of New York, represented in Senate and Assembly, That there shall be allowed and paid to the trustees of Columbia college, or their order, for the use of the institution, the sum of fifteen hundred pounds, for the purpose of enlarging its library, and the sum of two hundred pounds for a chemical apparatus; and the sum of twelve hundred pounds for the purpose of building a wall, necessary to support the grounds of the college, and the further sum of five thousand pounds for the purpose of erecting a hall and an additional wing to the college, pursuant to the original plan of the institution; and the treasurer is hereby authorized to pay the said respective sums out of such moneys as may be or may come into the treasury, of the annual revenue of the State, and which may not be appropriated for the purpose of supporting government, or satisfying claims against the State, or for compleating the sum of two hundred thousand pounds to be loaned in the several counties of this state, by virtue of the act, entitled, " An act for loaning moneys belonging to the State."

(Clause two, omitted.)

And be it further enacted, That the treasurer shall annually, for five years, unless otherwise directed by the legislature, pay to the trustees of Columbia college, or their order, out of the like moneys as above described, the sum of seven hundred and fifty pounds, to be applied to the payment of the salaries of such additional professors in the said college, as the said trustees shall think proper to appoint.

AN ACT FOR THE PAYMENT OF CERTAIN OFFICERS OF GOVERN-MENT AND OTHER CONTINGENT EXPENSES.

PASSED APRIL 11, 1796.

LAWS OF 1796, CHAP. 57.

After providing for payments to various State officers the act continues the grant of seven hundred and fifty pounds per annum, for two years, to Columbia College for the salaries of professors.

AN ACT RESPECTING UNION COLLEGE, AND FOR THE PURPOSES THEREIN MENTIONED.

PASSED MARCH 30, 1797.

LAWS OF 1797, CHAP. 65.

The Act confers certain powers upon the Trustees of Union College, and appropriates seven hundred and fifty dollars therefor, and grants five hundred dollars to Columbia College for the preservation of the anatomical museum, and the care thereof.

AN ACT TO AMEND THE ACT, ENTITLED, " AN ACT FOR THE ENCOURAGEMENT OF LITERATURE."

PASSED APRIL 3, 1802.

LAWS OF 1802, CHAPTER 105.

Whereas it appears, from a report of the surveyor-general, that the grant of a certain tract of land in the county of Washington, adjoining the south end of Lake George, to the regents of the university, in and by the act, entitled, " An act for the further encouragement of literature," interferes with the bounds of lands previously granted; and the regents having prayed for a grant of other lands adjoining the same, and in lieu thereof, to enable them the more effectually to fulfil the purposes for which the grant of those lands was intended: Therefore,

I. *Be it enacted by the People of the State of New-York, represented in Senate and Assembly,* That the said regents of the university, and their successors, shall be and hereby are vested with the seisin and possession of the lands hereafter described, belonging to the people of this state; that is to say, a certain tract of land in the county of Washington, adjoining the south end of Lake George, beginning on the east shore of the said lake, where the westerly bounds of a tract of two thousand acres, granted by letters patent to William Houghton, strikes the same, and running thence along the said Houghton's tract southerly and westerly to the northwest corner thereof, then with a straight line to the most westerly corner of a tract of two hundred acres granted by letters patent to John Jones, then along the southerly bounds thereof, to Lake George, and then along the same southerly, easterly, and northerly, to the place of beginning, containing one thousand seven hundred and twenty-four acres of land; and the former grant to the said regents, so far as the same included lands not herein described, shall be void.

II. *And be it further enacted,* That it shall be lawful for the said regents to grant and convey to the trustees of Columbia and Union colleges, and their successors, the lands above described, together with the lands at Ticonderoga and Crown Point already vested in the said regents, in such proportions as they shall deem just and reasonable, for the use of the said colleges respectively.

CHARTER OF 1810.

An Act relative to Columbia College in the city of New-York.   Passed March 23, 1810.
                                      Laws of 1810, Chapter 85.

Whereas the trustees of Columbia college, in the city of New-York, have represented, that sundry impediments to their trust, and to the interest of literature in the college, are found by experience from certain restrictions and defects in their charter, and have prayed relief, and that their charter, when amended, may be comprised in one act: Therefore,

I. BE *it enacted by the people of the State of New-York, represented in Senate and Assembly*, That John H. Livingston, Richard Varick, Brockholst Livingston, Abraham Beach, John Lawrence, Gershom Seixas, Richard Harison, John Watts, William Moor, Cornelius I. Bogart, John M. Mason, Edward Dunscomb, George C. Anthon, John N. Abeel, James Tillary, John H. Hobart, Benjamin Moore, Egbert Benson, Governeur Morris, Jacob Radcliff, Rufus King, Samuel Miller, Oliver Wolcott, and John B. Romeyn, the present trustees of the said college, and their successors, shall be and remain for ever here after, a body politic and corporate, in fact and in name, by the name of "The Trustees of Columbia College in the city of New-York," and by that name shall and may have continual succession for ever hereafter, and shall be able in law to sue and be sued, implead and be impleaded, answer and be answered unto, defend and be defended, in all courts and places whatsoever, and may have a common seal, and may change and alter the same at their pleasure, and also, shall be able in law to take by purchase, gift, grant, devise, or in any other manner, and to hold any real and personal estate whatsoever; *Provided always*, The clear yearly value of the real estate to be so acquired, shall not exceed the sum of twenty thousand dollars; and also that they and their successors shall have power to give, grant, bargain, sell, demise or otherwise dispose of, all or any part of the said real and personal estate, as to them shall seem best for the interest of the said college. (See Amendment, Laws of 1884, Chapter 65.)

II. *And be it further enacted*, That the said trustees, and their successors, shall forever hereafter have full power and authority to direct and prescribe the course of study, and the discipline to be observed in the said college, and also to select and appoint by ballot or otherwise, a president of the said college, who shall hold his office during good behaviour ; and such professor or professors, tutor or tutors to assist the president in the government and education of the students belonging to the said college, and such other officer or officers, as to the said trustees shall seem meet, all of whom shall hold their offices during the pleasure of the trustees: *Provided always*, That no such professor, tutor, or other assistant officer shall be trustee.

III. *And be it further enacted*, That if complaint shall be made in writing to the said trustees, or their successors, by any member of the said corporation of any misbehaviour in office by the president, it shall be lawful for the said trustees, or their successors, from time to time, upon examination, and such due proof of misbehaviour, to suspend or discharge such president, and to appoint another in his place.

IV. *And be it further enacted*, That eleven of the said trustees, lawfully convened, as is hereinafter directed, shall be a quorum for the despatch of all business, except for the disposal of real estate, or for the choice or removal of a president, for either of which purposes there shall be a meeting of at least thirteen trustees.

V. *And be it further enacted*, That the said trustees shall have full power and authority to elect by ballot their own chairman once in every year, or at such other periods as they shall prefer.

VI. *And be it further enacted*, That the said trustees shall also have power, by a majority of votes of the members present, to elect and appoint, upon the death, removal out of the state, or other vacancy of the place or places of any trustee or trustees, other or others, in his or their places or stead as often as such vacancy shall happen; and also to make and declare vacant the seat of any trustee who shall absent himself from five successive meetings of the board; and also to meet upon their own adjournment, and so often as they shall be summoned by their chairman, or in his absence by the senior trustee; whose seniority shall be accounted according to the order in which the said trustees are named in this act, and shall be elected hereafter; *Provided always*, That the said chairman or senior trustee shall not summon a meeting of the corporation unless required thereto in writing by three of the members; *And provided also*, That he cause notice of the time and place of the said meeting to be given in one or more of the public newspapers printed in the City of New-York, at least three days before such meeting: and that every member of the corporation resident in the city shall be previously advertised in writing of the time and place of every such meeting.

VII. *And be it further enacted*, That the said trustees and their successors, shall have power and authority to grant all such literary honors and degrees, as are usually granted by any university, college, or seminary of learning in this state, or in the United States; and in testimony of such grant to give suitable diplomas under their seal, and the signatures of the president and such professors, or tutors of the college, as they shall judge expedient; which diplomas shall entitle the possessors respectively to all the immunities and privileges which either by usage or statute are allowed to possessors of similar diplomas from any university, college, or seminary of learning.

VIII. *And be it further enacted*, That the said trustees, and their successors, shall have full power and authority to make all ordinances and bye-laws which to them shall seem expedient for carrying into effect the designs of their institution; *Provided always*, That such ordinances or bye-laws shall not make the religious tenets of any person a condition of admission to any privilege or office in the said college, nor be inconsistent with the constitution and laws of this state, nor with the constitution and laws of the United States.

IX. *And be it further enacted*, That all the real and personal estate whatsoever and wheresoever, which were formerly vested in the governors of the college of the province of New-York, in the city of New-York, in America, or in the trustees of Columbia college in the city of New-York, be and the same is hereby confirmed to and vested in the said trustees of Columbia college in the city of New-York, and their successors for ever, for the sole use and benefit of the said college; and that it shall and may be lawful to and for the said trustees, and their successors, to grant, bargain, sell, demise, improve and dispose of the same, as to them shall seem meet; *Provided always*, That the lands given land granted to the governors of the college of the province of New-York, in the city of New-York, in America, by the corporation heretofore styled, "The Rector and Inhabitants of the city of New-York, in communion of the Church of England, as by law established," on part whereof the said college is erected, shall not be granted for any greater term of time than sixty-three years. (See Amendment, Laws of 1852, Chapter 310.)

X. *And be it further enacted,* That the eighth, ninth, tenth, and eleventh sections of the act, entitled, " an act to institute an university within this state, and for other purposes therein mentioned," passed the thirteenth day of April, in the year of our Lord one thousand seven hundred and eighty-seven, be and the same are hereby repealed.

An Act to render the Provoost of Columbia College, in the City of New-York, eligible to be a Trustee thereof: Passed February 14, 1812.
Laws of 1812, Chapter 6.

Whereas, the trustees of Columbia college have, by their petition, prayed that the Provoost of the said college may be made eligible as a Trustee of said College:

Be it enacted by the People of the State of New-York, represented in Senate and Assembly, That it shall and may be lawful for the Provoost of Columbia College, in the city of New-York, for the time being, to be elected and act as a trustee of the said college, any thing contained in the act, entitled, " an act relative to Columbia College in the city of New-York," or in any other act or charter of the said college, to the contrary notwithstanding.

PETITION TO THE LEGISLATURE.

To the Honourable the Legislature of the State of New
York in Senate and Assembly convened:

The Memorial and Petition of the Trustees of Columbia
College in the City of New York, Respectfully Sheweth:

That your Memorialists have occupied themselves with great
solicitude, & as they believe, not without happy effect, in im-
proving the education of youth who resort to the Seminary
under their Care, They deem it neither arrogant in themselves,
nor disrespectful to others, to declare their firm conviction,
justified, as they suppose, by indisputable facts, that the whole
Instruction to be acquired in Columbia College will not suffer in
Comparison with that of any other american Colleges in its
present state, which they consider as an earnest of what they
may expect it will shortly become. But as the reasonable antici-
pations of your Memorialists are founded in no small degree
upon an increase of their pecuniary means, they address themselves with frankness & confidence to your honorable body for
such aid as shall enable them most efficiently to cherish the high
& important Interests committed to their charge.

Situated in the most important City of the State, an Object of
Curiosity & Remark to Strangers; & indispensable in its posi-
tion, to a large portion of the Students who must obtain a liberal
Education on the spot, or be deprived of it altogether, Columbia
College presents a Spectacle mortifying to its friends, humiliat-
ing to the City, and calculated to inspire opinions which it is
impossible your enlightened body would wish to countenance.

The foundation of a new wing to the Edifice, laid by the order
& under an Appropriation of your honorable body, has been for
Years, a heap of ruins solely for want of further public Assistance.

The Library of the College, which fell a sacrifice to the war
of independence, has never been replaced but in so slender a
degree as to make it a subject of ignominious Comparison with
the pre-eminence, in this Respect of other american Colleges.

The Philosophical Apparatus originally good, has been damaged by long use, & unavoidable Accident, and is now incompetent to the advanced State of physical Science.

There is no proper Apartment for the Reception of a decent Library. There is no Hall fit for the Performance of public Exercises. There is no astronomical Observatory which is of essential moment both to our commercial and military marine: a solid basis for such a Structure was laid at the same time with the foundation of the new wing and left unfinished for the same Cause.

𝕻our 𝕸emorialists are under the necessity of exacting, in two Instances the Labors of two Professorships from one Person, which renders the toil unreasonable and oppressive. They have found it due to the State of Science & and to public Opinion to institute a Professorship of Chemistry as a part of the academical Course, and have appointed a Professor without being able to give him any Compensation. They cannot employ Tutors to assist the Professors, an expedient found to be of eminent Utility in other Colleges. They cannot afford gratuitous Education to youth whose humble Circumstances debar them from its advantages, while their Talents and Virtues might render them Ornaments & blessings to their Country. They cannot erect buildings suitable for the Accommodation of the Students during the hours of Study, from which Circumstance much time is lost & injury sustained.

All these Difficulties & Embarrassments proceed solely from the Scantiness of their funds.

𝕻our 𝕸emorialists flatter themselves that no literary Institution in the State can offer to the contemplation of your honorable Body a case more fully entitled to legislative Sympathy and Succour.

𝕻our 𝕸emorialists are emboldened to hope that their Appeal to the magnanimity of your honorable Body will not be fruitless, especially when in addition to the preceding View, they respectfully add

1. That the patronage which Columbia College has received for a period of Thirty Years has been very limited & has not in the Aggregate amounted (if your Memorialists are correctly informed) to one fifth part of the benefactions made with the most praise worthy Munificence to a Kindred Institution.

2. That Columbia College was once in possession of landed property,* which if she still retained it, would be amply sufficient for her wants, & would save your Memorialists from the afflicting necessity of importuning your honorable body. That property was transferred by the State of New York, on great political Considerations to other hands. It was entirely lost to the College, and no Relief, under the privations which the loss occasioned, has hitherto been extended to her.

. 𝔜our 𝔐emorialists therefore pray that your honorable body will take the Premises into favorable Consideration, & grant such assistance therein as to your wisdom shall seem meet.

March 7, 1814.

RICHARD VARICK, *Chairman.*

AN ACT INSTITUTING A LOTTERY FOR THE PROMOTION OF LITERATURE, AND FOR OTHER PURPOSES.

PASSED APRIL 13, 1814.

LAWS OF 1814, CHAPTER 120.

𝔕ecites that "Whereas well regulated seminaries of learning are of immense importance to every country, and tend especially, by the diffusion of science and the promotion of morals, to defend and perpetuate the liberties of a free state," and provides for a lottery, the proceeds of which shall be paid to Union College, Hamilton College, the College of Physicians and Surgeons, and the Asbury African Church in the City of New York. The Act further provides:

VI. *And be it further enacted,* That all the right, title, and interest of the people of this state in and to all that certain piece or parcel of land, with the appurtenances, situate in the ninth ward of the city of New-York, known by the name of the Botanic Garden, and lately conveyed to the people of this state by David Hosack, with the appurtenances, be and the same is hereby granted to and vested in the trustees of Columbia college, in the city of New-York, their successors and assigns; but this grant is made upon the express condition, that the college establish-

---

* See Letters Patent, page 70.

ment shall be removed to the said tract of land hereby granted, or to lands adjacent thereto, within twelve years from this time; and if the said establishment shall not be so removed within the time above limited, then and from thenceforth, this grant shall cease and be void, and the premises hereby granted shall thereupon revert to the people of this state. (For Amendment, See Laws 1819, Chapter 19.)

VII. *And be it further enacted,* That the trustees of Columbia college shall, within three months from the time of the passage of this act, transmit to the trustees of each of the other colleges in this state, a list of the different kinds of plants, flowers, and shrubs in said garden; and within one year thereafter, the said trustees of Columbia college, shall deliver at the said garden, if required, at least one healthy exotic flower, shrub, or plant of each kind, of which they shall have more than one at the time of application, together with the jar or vessel containing the same, to the trustees of each of the other colleges of this state, who shall apply therefor. (Repealed by Laws 1819, Chapter 19.)

An Act relative to Columbia College, in the City of New-York. Passed February 19, 1819. Laws of 1819, Chapter 19.

Whereas, it is of the first importance in a free state, that seminaries of learning should be carefully protected, and, from time to time, receive the fostering aid of the legislature: *And whereas,* with these views, all the right, title and interest of the people of this state in a certain piece or parcel of land, situate in the ninth ward of the city of New-York, called "The Botanic Garden," was in and by an act of the legislature, entitled " an act instituting a lottery for the promotion of literature, and for other purposes," passed April 13th, 1814, given and granted to Columbia College, subject to certain conditions therein specified: *And whereas* the said grant has not been productive of the benefits intended by the said act: Therefore,

I. *BE it enacted by the People of the State of New-York, rep-*

resented in Senate and Assembly, That that part of the sixth section of the act, entitled, "an act instituting a lottery for the promotion of literature, and for other purposes," passed April 13th, 1814, which contains a condition to the grant made to the trustees of Columbia college, that the college establishment shall be removed to the tract of land thereby granted, or to the lands adjacent thereto, and the seventh section of the said act, be and the same are hereby repealed.

II. *And be it further enacted*, That the sum of ten thousand dollars be paid by the treasurer, on the warrant of the comptroller, to the trustees of Columbia College, out of any moneys not otherwise appropriated, to be applied by the said trustees as the interests of the said college may require.

An Act to amend an act, entitled "An Act relative to Columbia College, in the city of New-York," passed March 23, 1810. Passed April 15, 1852.

Laws of 1852, Chapter 310.

The People of the State of New York, represented in Senate and Assembly, do enact as follows :

§ I. The ninth section of the act entitled, "An act relative to Columbia College, in the city of New-York," passed March 23d, eighteen hundred and ten, is hereby amended, by adding at the end of said section the following words: "unless the consent of said grantors in writing, under their corporate seal, shall be first had and obtained to the disposal thereof, free from such restriction."

An Act to authorize the Trustees of Columbia College, in the City of New York, to take and hold certain real estate. Passed March 19, 1857.

Laws of 1857, Chapter 132.

The People of the State of New York, represented in the Senate and Assembly, do enact as follows:

§ I. The Trustees of Columbia College, in the City of New York, are hereby authorized to purchase and take, and to hold in fee simple, and dispose of a certain parcel of land, situated in the Nineteenth Ward of the City of New York, and bounded northerly by the southerly side of Fiftieth Street, southerly by the northerly side of Forty-ninth Street, easterly by a line parallel with and one hundred feet distant westerly from the westerly side of the Fourth Avenue, and westerly by a line parallel with and five hundred feet distant easterly from the easterly side of Fifth Avenue, or any part or parts thereof, and dispose of the proceeds for the use and purposes of said college.

§ II. This act shall take effect immediately.

An Act to Authorize the Trustees of Columbia College, in the City of New York, to take and hold certain real estate. Passed March 2, 1860.

Laws of 1860, Chapter 51.

The People of the State of New York represented in Senate and Assembly, do enact as follows :

§ I. 𝕿𝖍𝖊 𝕿𝖗𝖚𝖘𝖙𝖊𝖊𝖘 of Columbia College in the City of New York, are hereby authorized to purchase, and take and to hold in fee simple and dispose of such land, in addition to that which they were authorized to take and hold under the act entitled "An Act to Authorize the Trustees of Columbia College, in the City of New York to take and hold certain real estate" passed March nineteenth, eighteen hundred and fifty seven, as shall be situated in the City of New York, and shall, together with the land taken and held under the said act, be comprehended within the following bounds, to wit: the southerly side of Fiftieth Street, the westerly side of the Fourth Avenue, the Northerly side of Forty-ninth Street, and a line drawn parallel with Fourth Avenue and distant four hundred and fifty feet Westerly therefrom, or any part or parts thereof.

An Act relative to the law school of Columbia College. Passed April 7, 1860.

Laws of 1860, Chapter 202.

The People of the State of New York, represented in Senate and Assembly, do enact as follows :

𝕾𝖊𝖈𝖙𝖎𝖔𝖓 1. The professors in the Law School of Columbia College, and the law committee of the Trustees of said College, viz.: Samuel B. Ruggles, Hamilton Fish, Alexander W. Bradford, Gouverneur M. Ogden, George T. Strong and William Betts, and such persons as shall from time to time form such law committee, any three of whom, being counsellors at law, shall form a quorum upon whose examination and recommendation, as evidenced by the diploma of said College granted upon such recommendation, any graduate of said law school shall be admitted to practice as an attorney and counsellor at law in all the courts of this state. No diploma shall be sufficient for such admission which is given for any period of attendance upon said law school for a less term than eighteen months, but this period of eighteen months shall not apply to the members of the present senior class in said law school who may be admitted to practice as aforesaid upon the examination and recommendation of said committee, and upon the evidence of the diploma of the college.

SEC. 2. All acts and parts of acts inconsistent with this act are hereby repealed.

SEC. 3. This act shall take effect immediately.

NOTE.—Laws of 1877, Chapter 417, Section 1, sub-division 34, repeals so much of the foregoing act as requires the graduates therein specified to be admitted to practice upon the production of their diplomas; but Section 3, sub-division 17 of the same act provides that such repeal shall not affect the right of a person who is a student to be admitted at any time within one year after the passage of the repealing act. The period of exemption was further extended by the Laws of 1879, Chap. 35; Chap. 257; and Chap. 349; Laws of 1880, Chap. 58; and Laws of 1881, Chap. 25.

AN ACT IN RELATION TO COLUMBIA COLLEGE, IN THE CITY OF NEW YORK: PASSED MARCH 8, 1872.

LAWS 1872, CHAPTER 96.

The People of the State of New York, represented in Senate and Assembly, do enact as follows :

Section 1. The trustees of Columbia College, in the City of New York, are hereby authorized, from time to time, to purchase and take and hold in fee simple, any lands situate in the city of New York, for a new site or sites for the said college or for any of the schools or necessary buildings of the same, and to sell and convey any lands now held by said college, but no lands owned by said college shall be exempt from taxation, except such as are or may be in actual use as a site or sites for said college.

SEC. 2. This act shall take effect immediately.

An Act in relation to Columbia College in the City of
New York.   Passed March 28, 1884.
Laws of 1884, Chapter 65.

*The People of the State of New York, represented in Senate and
Assembly, do enact as follows :*

Section 1. The Trustees of Columbia College in the City of
New York are hereby authorized and empowered to take by
purchase, gift, grant, devise or any other manner, and to hold
any real estate which, when acquired, shall be used for, or the
income thereof shall be applied to, the proper conduct and support of the several departments of education heretofore established or hereafter to be established by such Trustees; and so
much of the proviso in the first section of the act entitled
"An Act relative to Columbia College in the City of New York,"
passed March 24, 1810, as limits the clear yearly value of the
real estate to be acquired by said Trustees to the sum of twenty
thousand dollars, is hereby repealed; provided, however, that
no lands owned by said college shall be exempt from taxation,
except such as are or may be in actual use as a site or sites for
said college; and provided further, that all devises and bequests
to said Trustees shall be subject to the provisions of chapter
three hundred and sixty of the laws of eighteen hundred and
sixty, entitled "An act relating to wills."   And provided
further that this act shall not be construed so as to affect any
devise made by any testator who shall have died before its
passage, nor the right of any heir at law or next of kin of such
testator.

SEC. 2. This act shall take effect immediately.

An Act to provide for the establishment of a botanic
garden and museum and arboretum, in Bronx Park in the
City of New York, and to incorporate the New York
Botanical Garden for carrying on the same.

PASSED APRIL 28, 1891.

LAWS OF 1891, CHAPTER 285.

*The People of the State of New York, represented in Senate and
    Assembly, do enact as follows:*

Section 1. Seth Low, Charles P. Daly, John S. Newbury,
Charles A. Dana, Addison Brown, Parke Godwin, Henry C.
Potter, Charles Butler, Hugh J. Grant, Edward Cooper,
Cornelius Vanderbilt, Nathaniel L. Britton, Morris K. Jessup,
J. Pierpont Morgan, Andrew Carnegie, Thomas F. Gilroy,
Eugene Kelly, Jr., Richard T. Auchmuty, D. O. Mills, Charles
F. Chandler, Louis Fitzgerald, Theodore W. Myers, William C.
Schermerhorn, Oswald Ottendorfer, Albert Gallup, Timothy F.
Allen, Henry R. Hoyt, William G. Choate, William H. Draper,
John S. Kennedy, Jesse Seligman, William L. Brown, David
Lydig, William E. Dodge, James A. Scrymser, Samuel Sloan,
William H. Robertson, Stephen P. Nash, Richard W. Gilder,
Thomas Hogg, Nelson Smith, Samuel W. Fairchild, Robert
Maclay, William H. S. Wood, George M. Olcutt, Charles F.
Cox, James R. Pitcher, Percy R. Pyne, and such persons as are
now, or may hereafter be associated with them, and their successors, are hereby constituted and created a body corporate by
the name of the New York Botanical Garden, to be located in
the city of New York, for the purpose of establishing and maintaining a botanical garden and museum and arboretum therein,
for the collection and culture of plants, flowers, shrubs and
trees, the advancement of botanical science and knowledge and
the prosecution of original researches therein and in kindred
subjects, for affording instruction in the same, for the prosecution and exhibition of ornamental and decorative horticulture
and gardening and for the entertainment, recreation and instruction of the people.

SEC. 2. Said corporation shall have all such corporate powers,
and may take and hold by gift, grant or devise all such real and
personal property as may be necessary and proper for carrying

out the purposes aforesaid, and for the endowment of the same, or any branch thereof, by adequate funds therefor.

Sec. 3. Said corporation may adopt a constitution and by-laws; make rules and regulations for the transaction of its business, the admission, suspension and expulsion of the associate members of said corporation, and for the number, election, terms and duties of its officers, subject to the provisions of this act; and may from time to time alter or modify its constitution, by-laws, rules and regulations, and shall be subject to the provisions of title three, of chapter eighteen, of the first part of the Revised Statutes.

Sec. 4. The affairs of the said corporation shall be managed and controlled by a board of managers as follows: The president of Columbia College, the professors of botany, of geology, and of chemistry therein, the president of the Torrey botanical club, and the president of the board of education of the city of New York, and their successors in office, shall be ex-officio members of said corporation and of the board of managers, and be known as the scientific directors; they shall have the management and control of the scientific and educational departments of said corporation and the appointment of the director-in-chief of said institution, who shall appoint his first assistant and the chief gardener, and be responsible for the general scientific conduct of the institution. All other business and affairs of the corporation, including its financial management, shall be under the control of the whole board of managers, which shall consist of the scientific directors, as herein provided, and of the mayor of the city of New York, the president of the board of commissioners of the department of public parks, and at least nine other managers to be elected by the members of the corporation. The first election shall be by ballot and held on a written notice of ten days, addressed by mail to each of the above-named incorporators, stating the time and place of election, and signed by at least five incorporators. Three of the managers so elected shall hold office for one year, three for two years, and three for three years. The term of office of the managers elected after the first election, save those elected to fill vacancies in unexpired terms, shall be three years; and three managers, and such others as may be needed to fill vacancies in

unexpired terms, shall be elected annually, pursuant to the by-
laws of the corporation. The number of elective managers may
be increased by vote of the corporation, whose terms and election shall be as above provided; and members may from time
to time be added to the scientific directors by a majority vote of
the scientific directors, approved by a majority vote of the whole
board of managers. The board of managers shall elect from
their number a president, secretary and treasurer, none of whom,
or of the board of managers, save the secretary and treasurer,
shall receive any compensation for his services. Nine corpora-
tors shall constitute a quorum at any meeting of the incorporators; but a less number may adjourn. (As amended by Laws
1894, Chapter 103.)

SEC. 5. Whenever the said corporation shall have raised, or
secured by subscription, a sum sufficient in the judgment of the
board of commissioners of the department of public parks in the
city of New York, for successfully establishing and prosecuting
the objects aforesaid, not less, however, than two hundred and
fifty thousand dollars within seven years from the passage of this
act, the said board of commissioners is hereby authorized and
directed to set apart and appropriate, upon such conditions as
to the said board may seem expedient, a portion of the Bronx
park, or of such other of the public parks in the city of New
York north of the Harlem river in charge of the said department
of parks as may be mutually agreed upon between the said
board of commissioners and the board of managers of said corporation in lieu of Bronx park, not exceeding two hundred and
fifty acres, for establishing and maintaining therein by the said
corporation a botanical garden and museum, including an herbarium and arboretum, and for the general purposes stated in the
first section of this act. And the said board of commissioners
is thereupon hereby authorized and directed to construct and
equip within the said grounds so allotted, according to plans
approved by them and by said board of managers, a suitable
fire-proof building for such botanical museum and herbarium,
with lecture-rooms and laboratories for instruction, together
with other suitable buildings for the care and culture of tender
or other plants, indigenous or exotic, at an aggregate cost not
exceeding the bonds hereinafter authorized to be issued by the

city of New York; the use of said buildings upon completion to be transferred to said corporation for the purposes stated in this act. And for the purpose of providing means therefor, it shall be the duty of the comptroller of the city of New York, upon being thereto requested by said commissioners, and upon being authorized thereto by the board of estimate and apportionment, to issue and sell at not less than their par value bonds or stock of the mayor, aldermen and commonalty of the city of New York, in the manner now provided by law, payable from taxation, aggregating the sum of five hundred thousand dollars, bearing interest at a rate not exceeding three per centum per annum, and to be redeemed within a period of time not longer than thirty years from the date of their issue. (As amended by Laws 1894, Chapter 103.)

Sec. 6. The grounds set apart as above provided, shall be used for no other purpose than authorized by this act; and no intoxicating liquors shall be sold or allowed thereon. For police purposes, and for the maintenance of proper roads and walks, the said grounds shall remain subject at all times to the control of the said board of commissioners of the department of parks; but otherwise after the suitable laying out of the same, and the construction of proper roads and walks therein by the department of parks, the said grounds and buildings shall be under the management and control of the said corporation. The said grounds shall be open and free to the public daily, including Sundays, subject to such restrictions only as to hours as the proper care, culture and preservation of the said garden may require; and its educational and scientific privileges shall be open to all alike, male and female, upon such necessary regulations, terms and conditions as shall be prescribed by the managers of those departments.

Sec. 7. This act shall take effect immediately.

AN ACT IN RELATION TO CERTAIN AVENUES AND STREETS IN
THE CITY OF NEW YORK.   PASSED APRIL 5, 1892.
            LAWS OF 1892, CHAPTER 230.

*The People of the State of New York, represented in Senate and
Assembly, do enact as follows :*

§ection 1. It shall be the duty of the counsel to the corporation and the board of street openings of the city of New York,
to take the necessary means and proceedings to open the following streets in said city: One Hundred and Twenty-first Street,
from Amsterdam Avenue to the Boulevard.   No street, road or
avenue shall hereafter be laid out or opened through or upon
any part of the lands and premises lying between Amsterdam
Avenue and the Boulevard and One Hundred and Sixteenth
and One Hundred and Twentieth streets, in the city of New
York, whenever and so long as the same shall be owned or
occupied for educational purposes by the trustees of Columbia
College in the city of New York; provided, however, that
nothing in this section contained shall be construed to interfere with the opening of One Hundred and Sixteenth street
after January first, eighteen hundred and ninety-four, and that
the said, the trustees of Columbia College in the city of New
York, shall dedicate without claim or award for damages the
northerly one-half of the land required for said street so far as
the said street forms the southerly boundary of the aforesaid
first mentioned lands and premises, and for street purposes a
strip of land forty feet in width on the southerly side of One
Hundred and Twentieth street, from Amsterdam avenue to the
Boulevard.

§ 2. All the laws now in force in said city in relation to the
opening and improvement of streets and avenues, and the payment and the assessment of the expense thereof shall apply to
the said streets; provided, however, that nothing contained in
any act shall authorize the discontinuance of any proceedings
which may be taken to open the said streets.

§ 3. All motions and applications for the appointment of commissioners in said proceedings may be made at any special term
of the supreme court held in and for the city and county of New
York.   Upon the coming in and confirmation by the court of the

report of such commissioners, the commissioner of public works shall proceed and actually open, grade, regulate, pave and improve said streets.

§ 4. All acts and parts of acts heretofore passed, so far as the same interfere or are inconsistent with this act, are hereby repealed.

§ 5. This act shall take effect immediately.

AN ACT TO PERMIT THE UNION OF THE COLLEGE OF PHY-
SICIANS AND SURGEONS IN THE CITY OF NEW YORK WITH THE
TRUSTEES OF COLUMBIA COLLEGE IN THE CITY OF NEW YORK.
PASSED MARCH 24, 1891.
LAWS 1891, CHAP. 101.

*The People of the State of New York, represented in Senate and
Assembly, do enact as follows :*

Section 1. The trustees of the College of Physicians and
Surgeons in the city of New York, having arranged with
Columbia college in said city to assume the instruction now
given by the said College of Physicians and Surgeons as a
department of the work of Columbia college, are hereby
authorized and empowered to grant, convey, assign and transfer
all real and personal property of which they as such trustees are
seized or possessed to the trustees of Columbia college, in the
city of New York, upon such terms, conditions or limitations as
may be agreed upon between the two institutions.

SEC. 2. The regents of the university of the state of New
York, upon being satisfied that the trustees of the College of
Physicians and Surgeons have conveyed and transferred all
their property, pursuant to the authority hereinbefore conferred,
may accept a surrender of the charter heretofore granted by the
said regents to the said College of Physicians and Surgeons,
and forever discharge the said trustees from their trusts in the
premises.

SEC. 3. This act shall take effect immediately.

An Act to ratify the union of the College of Physicians and Surgeons in the city of New York with the Trustees of Columbia College in the city of New York, and to define certain rights, duties and powers of the dean of the medical faculty of Columbia College.

PASSED MARCH 6, 1894.

LAWS 1894, CHAP. 97.

The People of the State of New York, represented in Senate ana Assembly, do enact as follows :

Section 1. The union of the College of Physicians and Surgeons in the city of New York with the Trustees of Columbia College in the city of New York, pursuant to chapter one hundred and one of the laws of eighteen hundred and ninety-one, entitled "An act to permit the union of the College of Physicians and Surgeons in the city of New York with the Trustees of Columbia College in the city of New York," is hereby ratified and confirmed; and the Trustees of Columbia college are hereby substituted as successors to and as trustees in the place and stead of the trustees of the College of Physicians and Surgeons for the execution of any and all trusts now vested in or which may hereafter devolve upon the Trustees of the College of Physicians and Surgeons; and the dean of the medical faculty of Columbia College and his successors are hereby declared to be the successors in office of the president of the managing board of the College of Physicians and Surgeons in the city of New York, with all the rights, powers and duties heretofore conferred upon or vested in the president of the managing board of the College of Physicians and Surgeons and his successors in office by chapter four of the laws of eighteen hundred and sixty-four, entitled "An act to incorporate the Roosevelt Hospital in the city of New York," or by any other act of the Legislature or by deed or will.

SEC. 2. This act shall take effect immediately.

Official Documents.

LEASE BY TRINITY CHURCH OF A PORTION OF THE KING'S FARM.

This Indenture made the twelfth day of May in the twenty-eighth year of the reign of our Sovereign Lord George the Second by the Grace of God of Great Britain, France and Ireland King, Defender of the Faith, &c. and in the year of our Lord one thousand seven hundred and fifty-five BETWEEN the Rector and Inhabitants of the City of New York in communion of the Church of England as by law established* of the one part and the Governors of the College of the Province of New York in the City of New York in America of the other part Witnesseth that the said Rector and Inhabitants of the City of New York in communion of the Church of England as by law established for and in consideration of the sum of ten shillings to them in hand paid by the Governors of the College of the Province of New York in the City of New York in America at or before the sealing and delivery of these presents, the receipt whereof is hereby acknowledged HAVE bargained, Sold and Demised and by these Presents DO Bargain, Sell and Demise unto the said Governors of the College of the Province of New York in the City of New York in America, All that certain Piece or Parcell of ground Situate, lying and being on the West side of the Broadway in the West ward of the City of New York, fronting easterly to Church Street between Barclay Street and Murray Street four hundred and forty foot and from thence running Westerly between and along the said Barclay Street and Murray Street to the North River and also the use of a street called Robinson Street from the Middle of the said Land, easterly to the Broadway of Ninty foot in

---

* The corporate title, " The Rector and Inhabitants of the City of New York in Communion of the Church of England," was changed to " The Rector and Inhabitants of the City of New York in Communion of the Protestant Episcopal Church in the State of New York," by Chapter 66 of the Laws of 1788, and was again changed to " The Rector, Church Wardens and Vestrymen of Trinity Church in the City of New York," by Chapter 1 of the Laws of 1814.

breadth, together with all and singular the Wells, Waters, Fences, Ways, easements, Profitts, Commodities and Appurtenances whatsoever to the aforesaid piece or Parcell of Ground belonging or in anywise appertaining and the Reversion and Reversions, remainder and remainders, rents, Issues and profitts thereof 𝖙𝖔 𝖍𝖆𝖛𝖊 𝖆𝖓𝖉 𝖙𝖔 𝖍𝖔𝖑𝖉 the said piece or parcell of ground and premises with the appurtenances herein before mentioned and discribed and intended to be hereby demised with their and every of their appurtenances and the use of the said Street of ninty foot in breadth unto the said Governors of the College of the Province of New York in the City of New York in America and their successors from the day next before the day of the date of these Presents for and during the Term of one whole year from thence next ensuing and fully to be compleat and ended Yielding and paying therefore unto the said Rector and Inhabitants of the City of New York in communion of the Church of England as by law established and their successors the rent of one pepper corn on the last day of the said Term if demanded   To the intent that by virtue of these Presents and of the Statute for transferring of uses into Possession the said Governors of the College of the Province of New York in the City of York in America may be in the Actual Possession of the said hereby bargained Premises with their appurtenances and be thereby enabled to accept and take a Grant and Release of the reversion & inheritance thereof to them and their successors for ever.

𝕴𝖓 𝖜𝖎𝖙𝖓𝖊𝖘𝖘 𝖜𝖍𝖊𝖗𝖊𝖔𝖋 to the one part of these Present Indentures remaining with the said Governors of the College of the Province of New York in the City of New York in America the said Rector and Inhabitants of the City of New York in communion of the Church of England as by law established have caused their Seal to be affixed and to the other part thereof remaining with the said Rector and Inhabitants of the City of New York in communion of the Church of England as by law established they the said Governors of the College of the Province of New York in the City of New York in America have caused their Seal to be affixed the Day and year first above written.

[SEAL OF THE CORPORATION.]

RELEASE BY TRINITY CHURCH OF A PORTION OF
THE KING'S FARM.

𝕿𝖍𝖎𝖘 𝕴𝖓𝖉𝖊𝖓𝖙𝖚𝖗𝖊 Made the Thirteenth day of May in the Twenty-eighth year of the reign of our Sovereign Lord George the Second by the Grace of God of Great Britain, France and Ireland King, Defender of the Faith, &c. and in the year of our Lord one thousand seven hundred and fifty-five BETWEEN the Rector and Inhabitants of the City of New York in communion of the Church of England as by law established of the one part, and the Governors of the College of the Province of New York in the City of New York in America of the other part 𝖂𝖎𝖙𝖓𝖊𝖘𝖘𝖊𝖙𝖍 that the said Rector and Inhabitants of the City of New York in communion of the Church of England as by law established as well as for the encouraging and promoting the founding, erecting and establishing a College in the said Province of New York for the education and instruction of youth in the Liberal Arts and sciences as for and in consideration of the sum of ten shillings to them in hand paid by the Governors of the College of the Province of New York in the City of New York in America at or before the sealing and delivery of these Presents, the receipt whereof is hereby acknowledged and for divers other good causes and considerations them thereunto moving They the said Rector and Inhabitants of the City of New York in communion of the Church of England as by law established HAVE Granted, bargained, sold, aliened, remised, released and confirmed and by these Presents DO grant, bargain, sell, alien, remise, release and confirm unto the said Governors of the College of the Province of New York in the City of New York in America, in their actual possession now being by virtue of a Bargain and Sale to them thereof made by the said Rector and inhabitants of the city of New York in communion of the Church of England as by law established by Indenture bearing date the day next before the day of the date of these presents and of the Statute for transferring of uses into possession and to their successors forever 𝕬𝖑𝖑 𝖙𝖍𝖆𝖙 certain piece or parcell of ground

66

Situate, lying and being on the West side of the Broadway in the West ward of the City of New York fronting easterly to Church Street between Barclay Street and Murray Street four hundred and forty foot and from thence running westerly between and along said Barclay Street and Murray Street to the North river and also the use of a Street called Robinson Street from the Middle of the said Land easterly to the Broadway of Ninty foot in breadth together will all and singular the Wells, Waters, Fences, ways, easements, profitts, Commodities and appurtenances whatsoever to the aforesaid piece or parcell of ground belonging or in anywise appertaining and the reversion and reversions remainder and remainders, rents, issues and profitts thereof and all the Estate, Right, Title, Interest, property, possession, claim and demand whatsoever of them the said Rector and Inhabitants of the City of New York in communion of the Church of England as by law established of in or to the same and every part and parcell thereof to have and to hold the said piece or parcell of Ground and Premises with the appurtenances hereinbefore mentioned and described and intended to be hereby granted and released with their and every of their appurtenances and the use of the said street of ninety foot in breadth unto the said Governors of the College of the Province of New York in the City of New York in America and their successors forever, Provided nevertheless and this present grant and release is upon this express condition that the President of the said College forever for the time being shall be Member of and in communion with the Church of England as by law established and that the Morning and Evening Service in the said College be the Liturgy of the said Church or such a Collection of Prayers out of the said Liturgy with a Collect peculiar for the said College as shall be agreed upon and approved of by the President and Governors of the said College and that upon failure thereof this present grant and release shall cease, determine and be utterly void and of none effect to all intents and purposes as if the same had never been made, anything herein contained to the contrary notwithstanding. And the said Rector and Inhabitants of the City of New York in communion of the Church of England as by law established for themselves and their successors do

hereby covenant, promise, grant and agree to and with the said
Governors of the College of the Province of New York in the City
of New York in America and their successors in manner and form
following (that is to say) that the said hereby bargained &
Released Premises and every part and parcell thereof now are
and at all times hereafter (untill failure be made in performance
of the Provisoe and Condition aforesaid) shall be, remain and
continue free and clear and freely and clearly acquitted and discharged of and from all manner of former and other gifts,
grants and mortgages, titles, troubles, charges and incumbrances
whatsoever had, made and done, committed or willingly suffered
by them the said Rector and Inhabitants in the City of New
York in communion of the Church of England as by law established or any other person or persons whatsover claiming by
from or under them AND that they the said Governors of the
College of the Province of New York in the City of New York in
America and their successors shall and may from time to time
and at all times hereafter until failure be made in the Performance of the Provisoe and condition aforesaid have hold,
occupy, possess and enjoy the said hereby bargained and released
premises and every part thereof without any lett, suit, trouble,
molestation or hindrance of them the said Rector and inhabitants of the City of New York in communion of the Church of
England as by law established, their successors or assigns or any
other person or persons whatsoever claiming by from or under
them.

In witness whereof to one part of these Present Indentures
remaining with the said Governors of the College of the Province of New York in the City of New York in America the said
Rector and Inhabitants of the City of New York in communion
of the Church of England as by law established, have caused
their seal to be affixed and to the other part thereof remaining
with the said Rector and Inhabitants of the City of New York in
communion of the Church of England as by law established they
the said Governors of the College of the Province of New York
in the City of New York in America have caused their seal to be
affixed the Day and year first above written.

[SEAL OF THE CORPORATION.]

PROSPECTUS OF THE COLLEGE.

NEW YORK, May 31, 1754.

ADVERTISEMENT.

𝕿𝖔 𝖘𝖚𝖈𝖍 𝕻𝖆𝖗𝖊𝖓𝖙𝖘 as have now (or expect to have) Children pre-pared to be educated in the College of New-York.

I. As the Gentlemen who are appointed by the Assembly, to be Trustees of the intended Seminary or College of New-York, have thought fit to appoint me to take the Charge of it, and have concluded to set up a Course of Tuition in the learned Lan-guages, and in the Liberal Arts and Sciences: They have judged it advisible that I should publish this *Advertisement*, to inform such as have Children ready for a College Education, that it is proposed to begin Tuition upon the first Day of *July* next, at the *Vestry Room* in the new *School-House*, adjoining to *Trinity-Church* in *New-York*, which the Gentlemen of the Vestry are so good as to favour them with the Use of it in the Interim, till a con-venient Place may be built.

II. The lowest Qualifications they have judged requisite in order to Admission into the said College, are as follows, *viz.* That they be able to read well, and write a good legible Hand; and that they be well versed in the Five first Rules in *Arithmetic*, i. e. as far as *Division* and *Reduction ;* And as to *Latin* and *Greek*, That they have a good Knowledge in the *Grammars*, and be able to make grammatical *Latin*, and both in construing and pars-ing, to give a good Account of two or three of the first select Orations of *Tully*, and of the first Books of *Virgil's Aeneid*, and some of the first Chapter of the *Gospel of St. John*, in *Greek*. In these Books therefore they may expect to be examined; but higher Qualifications must hereafter be expected: and if there be any of the higher Classes in any College, or under private Instruction, that incline to come hither, they may expect Admis-sion to proportionably higher Classes here.

III. And that People may be the better satisfied in sending their Children for Education to this College, it is to be under-stood that as to Religion, there is no Intention to impose on the

Scholars, the peculiar Tenets of any particular Sect of Christians; but to inculcate upon their tender Minds, the great Principles of Christianity and Morality, in which true Christians of each Denomination are generally agreed. And as to the daily Worship in the College Morning and Evening, it is proposed that it should, ordinarily, consist of such a Collection of Lessons, Prayers and Praises of the Liturgy of the Church, as are, for the most Part, taken out of the Holy Scriptures, and such as are agreed on by the Trustees, to be in the best Manner expressive of our common Christianity; and, as to any peculiar Tenets, everyone is left to judge freely for himself, and to be required only to attend constantly at such Places of Worship, on the Lord's Day, as their Parents or Guardians shall think fit to order or permit.

IV. The chief Thing that is aimed at in this College is, to teach and engage the Children to *know God in Jesus Christ*, and to love and serve him, in all *Sobriety, Godliness,* and *Righteousness* of Life, with a *perfect Heart, and* a *willing Mind;* and to train them up in all virtuous Habits, and all such useful Knowledge as may render them creditable to their Families and Friends, Ornaments to their Country and useful to the public Weal in their Generations. To which good Purposes, it is earnestly desired, that their Parents, Guardians and Masters, would train them up from their Cradles, under strict Government, and in all Seriousness, Virtue and Industry, that they may be qualified to make orderly and tractable Members of this Society;—and, above all, that in order hereunto, they be very careful themselves, to set them good Examples of true Piety and Virtue in their own Conduct. For as Examples have a very powerful Influence over young Minds, and especially those of their Parents, in vain are they solicitous for a good Education for their Children, if they themselves set before them Examples of Impiety and Profanness, or of any sort of Vice whatsoever.

V. And, *lastly,* a serious, *virtuous,* and *industrious* Course of Life, being first provided for, it is further the Design of this College, to instruct and perfect the Youth in the Learned Languages, and in the Arts of *reasoning* exactly, of *writing* correctly, and *speaking* eloquently; and in the Arts of *numbering* and *measuring;* of *Surveying* and *Navigation,* of *Geography* and *History,*

of *Husbandry, Commerce* and *Government*, and in the Knowledge of
all Nature in the *Heavens* above us, and in the *Air, Water* and
Earth around us, and the various kinds of *Meteors, Stones, Mines*
and *Minerals, Plants* and *Animals*, and of every Thing *useful* for
the Comfort, the Convenience and Elegance of Life, in the
chief *Manufactures* relating to any of these Things : And, finally,
to lead them from the Study of Nature to the Knowledge of
themselves, and of the God of Nature, and their Duty to him,
themselves, and one another, and every Thing that can contribute to their true Happiness, both here and hereafter.

Thus much, *Gentlemen*, it was thought proper to advertise you
of, concerning the Nature and Design of this College : And I
pray God, it may be attended with all the Success you can wish,
for the best Good of the rising Generations; to which, (while I
continue here), I shall willingly contribute my Endeavours to the
Utmost of my Power.

Who am, Gentlemen, Your real Friend And most humble
Servant

Samuel Johnson.

N. B. The Charge of the Tuition is established by the Trustees to be only 25s. for each Quarter.

The foregoing advertisement appeared in the " New-York
Mercury," No. 95, and also in the " New-York Gazette; or
Weekly Post Boy " of June 3, 1754, No. 592. The following
notice was published in the latter journal on July 1, 1754, No.
596 :

𝕿𝖍𝖎𝖘 𝖎𝖘 𝖙𝖔 𝖆𝖈𝖖𝖚𝖆𝖎𝖓𝖙 whom it may concern that I shall attend
at the Vestry Room in the School-House, near the English
Church, on Tuesdays and Thursdays every week, between the
Hours of Nine and Twelve, to examine such as offer themselves
to be admitted into the College.

Samuel Johnson.

LETTERS PATENT OF THE TOWNSHIP OF KINGSLAND.

𝕲𝖊𝖔𝖗𝖌𝖊 𝖙𝖍𝖊 𝖙𝖍𝖎𝖗𝖉, by the grace of God, of Great Britain, France and Ireland king defender of the faith and so forth.

TO all whom these presents shall come 𝖌𝖗𝖊𝖊𝖙𝖎𝖓𝖌.

𝖂𝖍𝖊𝖗𝖊𝖆𝖘 the Governors of the College of the Province of New York in the city of New York in America by their humble petition presented unto our late trusty and well beloved Sir Henry Moore, Baronet then our Captain General and Governor-in-chief of our said Province and read in our Council for our said Province on the fourth day of February which was in the year of our Lord one thousand seven hundred and sixty seven, did set forth among other things, that the petitioners being desirous of extending and rendering as beneficial as possible the laudable institution committed to their care which had been distinguished by the countenance, protection and liberality of our said late captain general and governor in chief's predecessors, had been at some pains in discovering a tract of vacant land in hopes that our said late captain general and governor in chief from a consideration that there was a similar provision for learning in other colonies might be induced to appropriate the same for the better support of an establishment, in the prosperity of which they conceived the public to be deeply interested. That there was a tract of land which tho' very distant and uncultivated, they hoped and under proper improvement might contribute to this end. Situate on the west side of Connecticut river within our said Province and called and known by the name of Dasham, bounded to the eastward by a tract of land then lately petitioned for and to be called Gageborough; to the southward by a tract of land commonly called or known by the name of Tunbridge, to the westward by vacant land, and to the northward by a tract of land then lately petitioned for under the name of Chatham, and extending so far westward as to comprehend the quantity of twenty-five thousand acres. And therefore the petitioners do humbly pray that our said late captain general and governor in chief would be favorably pleased by our letters pat-

72

ent to grant unto them and their successors the tract of land
above described and that the same might be erected into a
township with the usual privileges WHICH PETITION having been
referred to a committee of our Council for our said Province
our said Council did afterwards on the twelfth day of the
same month of February in pursuance of the report of the
said committee humbly advise and consent that our said late
captain general and governor in chief should grant the prayer
hereof anð wbereas the said petitioners by their farther petition presented unto our trusty and well beloved Cadwallader
Colden, esquire, our lieutenant governor and commander in chief
of our said Province and read in our said Council on the seventh
day of February now last past did among other things set forth,
that on the thirteenth day of May which was in the said year of
our Lord one thousand seven hundred and sixty seven a certain
other tract of land was advised to be granted to Nathaniel
Marston and his associates situate on the west side of Connecticut river bounded easterly by a tract of land commonly called
or known by the name of Corinth and southerly by the above
mentioned tract of land known by the name of Dasham, northerly by a line beginning at the west line of the said tract of
land known by the name of Corinth at the distance of about
four miles and an half from the southwest corner of the said
tract of land known by the name of Corinth and running
parallel to the north boundary line of the said tract of land
known by the name of Dasham and westerly by a line from the
north line of the said tract of land known by the name of
Dasham continued westward to the said parallel line and at
such a distance from the said tract of land known by the name
of Corinth and parallel thereto as to comprehend twenty-four
thousand acres. That the said Nathaniel Marston and his
associates had relinquished their claim thereto, intending with
the consent of the petitioners to apply for a grant of the tract
first above described in lieu thereof, that neither of the said
tracts of land though within the limits formerly claimed by the
government of New Hampshire had ever been patented or
granted under that government and therefore the petitioners
did humbly pray that our said lieutenant governor and commander in chief would be favorably pleased to grant to them

and their successors the said tract of twenty-four thousand
acres of land instead of the tract prayed for by them in their
said first recited petition and that the said tract of twenty-four
thousand acres might be erected into a township by the name of
Kingsland with the usual privileges granted to other townships
within our said Province.   On reading and due consideration
of which last recited petition our Council of our said Province
did humbly advise and consent that our said lieutenant governor
and commander in chief should by our letters patent grant to
the said petitioners and their successors for ever the tract of
twenty-four thousand acres of land last described as aforesaid
under the quit rent, provisoes, limitations and restrictions prescribed by our Royal instructions.   And that the said tract of
twenty-four thousand acres of land should be erected into a
township by the name of Kingsland with the usual privileges
granted to other townships within our Province of New
York.   In pursuance whereof and in obedience to our said
Royal instructions our commissioners appointed for the setting out all lands to be granted within our said Province
have set out for the said petitioners All that certain tract
or parcel of land within our province of New York situate,
lying and being in the county of Albany on the west side of
Connecticut river beginning at a beech tree marked with the
letters WK NWcorner PM, EW, for the southwest corner of a
tract of land called Corinth and runs thence along part of the
west bounds of the last mentioned tract north thirty degrees
east three hundred and sixty chains to a hard maple tree, having some large stones laid around it and a beech tree twenty
five links west of the said maple tree marked with the letters
and figures PM, EW 1767.   Then from the aforesaid hard maple
tree north fifty seven degrees west seven hundred and one
chains; then south thirty degrees west three hundred and sixty
chains; then south fifty seven degrees east seven hundred and
one chains to the place where this tract first began containing
twenty four thousand acres of land and the usual allowance for
highways and in setting out the said tract of twenty four thousand acres of land our said commissioners have had regard to
the profitable and unprofitable acres and have taken care that
the length of the said tract of land doth not extend along the

banks of any river otherwise than is conformable to our said
Royal instructions as by a certificate thereof under their hands
bearing date the second day of this instant month of March
and entered on record in our secretary's office for our said Province may more fully appear which said tract of. land set out as
aforesaid according to our said Royal instructions. We being
willing to grant to the said petitioners their successors assigns
for ever with the several privileges with the several privileges
and powers hereinbefore mentioned. 𝕶𝖓𝖔𝖜 𝖓𝖊 that of our
special grace certain knowledge and meer motion we have given
granted, ratified and confirmed and do by these presents for us,
our heirs and successors give, grant, ratify and confirm unto
them the Governors of the College of the Province of New York
in the city of New York in America their successors and assigns
for ever all that the tract or parcel of land aforesaid set out
abutted, bounded and described in manner and form as above
mentioned, together with all and singular the tenements, hereditaments, emoluments and appurtenances thereunto belonging
or appertaining and also all our Estate, Right, Title, Interest,
possession, Claim and Demand whatsoever of, in and to the same
lands and premises and every part and parcel thereof and the
reversion and reversions, remainder and remainders, rents, issues
and profits thereof and every part and parcel thereof except and
always reserved out of this our present grant unto us, our heirs
and successors for ever all mines of Gold and Silver and also all
white or other sorts of pine trees fit for masts, of the growth
of twenty-four inches diameter and upwards of twelve inches
from the earth for masts for the royal navy of us, our heirs
and successors 𝖙𝖔 𝖍𝖆𝖛𝖊 𝖆𝖓𝖉 𝖙𝖔 𝖍𝖔𝖑𝖉 the said tract or parcel of
land, tenements, hereditaments and premises by these presents
granted, ratified and confirmed and every part and parcel
thereof with their and every of their appurtenances (except
as is hereinbefore excepted) unto them the Governors of the
College of the Province of New York in the City of New York
in America their successors and assigns, to the only proper
use and behoof of them the Governors of the College of the
Province of New York in the City of New York in America their
successors and assigns for ever, to be holden of us, our heirs
and successors in free and common socage as of our manor of

East Greenwich in our county of Kent within our Kingdom of Great Britain YIELDING, rendering and paying therefore yearly and every year for ever unto us, our heirs and successors at our custom house in our city of New York unto our or their collector or receiver general there for the time being, on the feast of the Annunciation of the Blessed Virgin Mary, commonly called Lady Day, the yearly rent of two shillings and six pence sterling for each and every hundred acres of the above granted lands and so in proportion for any lesser quantity thereof, saving and except for such part of the said lands allowed for highways as above mentioned in lieu and stead of all other rents services, dues, duties and demands whatsoever for the hereby granted lands and premises or any part thereof AND we do of our especial grace certain knowledge and meer motion create, erect and constitute the tract or parcel of land herein granted and every part and parcel thereof a township for ever hereafter to be continue and remain and by the name of KINGSLAND for ever hereafter to be called and known AND for the better and more easily carrying on and managing the public affairs and business of the said township our royal will and pleasure is and we do hereby for us, our heirs and successors give and grant to the inhabitants of the said township all the powers, authorities, privileges and advantages heretofore given and granted to, or legally enjoyed by, all any or either our other townships within our said Province. And we also ordain and establish, that there shall be for ever hereafter in the said township two assessors, one treasurer, two overseers of the highways, two overseers of the poor, one collector and four constables elected and chosen out of the inhabitants of the said township yearly and every year on the first Tuesday in May at the most public place in the said township by the majority of the freeholders thereof then and there met and assembled for that purpose; hereby declaring, that wheresoever the first election in the said township shall be held, the future elections shall for ever thereafter be held in the same place, as near as may be, and giving and granting to the said officers so chosen power and authority to exercise their said several and respective offices during one whole year from such election and until others are legally chosen and elected in their room and stead as fully and amply as any the like officers have or legally may use or exercise their offices in our said Province. And in case any or either of the said officers of the said township should die or remove from the said township before the time of their annual service shall be expired, or refuse to act in the offices for which they shall respectively be chosen, then our royal will and pleasure further is and we do hereby direct, ordain and require the freeholders of the said township to meet at the place where the annual election shall be held for the said township and choose other or others of the said inhabitants of the said township in the place and stead of him or them so dying, removing or refusing to act, within forty days next after such contingency. And to prevent any undue election in this case, we do hereby ordain and require, that upon every vacancy in the office of assessors, the treasurer and in either of the other offices the assessors of the said township shall within ten days next after any such vacancy first happens appoint the day for such election and give public notice thereof in writing under his or their hands, by affixing such notice on the church door or other most public place in the said township, at least ten days before the day appointed for such election, and in default thereof we do hereby require the officer or officers of the said township or the survivor of them who in the order they are hereinbefore mentioned shall next succeed him or them so making default within ten days next after such default, to appoint the day for such election and to give notice thereof as aforesaid; hereby giving and granting that such person or persons as shall be so chosen by the majority of such of the freeholders of the said township as shall meet in manner hereby directed shall have, hold, exercise and enjoy the office or offices to which he or they shall be so elected and chosen from the time of such election until the first Tuesday in May then next following, and until other or others be legally chosen in his or their place and stead, as fully as the person or persons in whose place he or they shall be chosen might or could have done by virtue of these presents. And we do hereby will and direct, that this method shall for ever hereafter be used for the filling up all vacancies that shall happen in any or either of the said offices between the annual elections above directed PROVIDED always and upon condition, nevertheless, that if our said grantees their

successors or assigns shall not within three years next after the
date of this our present grant settle on the said tract of land
hereby granted so many families as shall amount to one family
for every thousand acres of the same tract, or if they our said
grantees their successors or assigns shall not also within three
years to be computed as aforesaid plant and effectually cultivate
at the least three acres for every fifty acres of such of the
hereby granted lands as are capable of cultivation, or if they
our said grantees their successors or assigns or any other person
or persons by their, or any of their privity, consent or procure-
ment shall fell, cut down or otherwise destroy any of the pine
trees by these presents reserved to us, our heirs and successors
or hereby intended so to be without the royal license of us, our
heirs, or successors for so doing first had and obtained, that then
and in any of these cases this our present grant and every thing
hereinbefore contained, shall cease and be absolutely void and
the lands and premises hereby granted shall revert to and vest
in us, our heirs and successors, as if this our present grant concerning the same had not been made any thing hereinbefore
contained to the contrary in any wise notwithstanding.

Provided further and upon condition also nevertheless and we
do hereby for us, our heirs and successors direct and appoint
that this our present grant shall be registered and entered on
record with in six months from the date thereof in our secretary's office in our city of New York in our said Province in one
of the books of patents there remaining and that a docquet
thereof shall be also entered in our auditors office there for our
said province and that in default thereof this our present grant
shall be void and of none effect, any thing before in these presents contained to the contrary thereof in any wise notwithstanding **and whereas** by the charter of our late royal grandfather
King George the second under his great seal of the said Province of New York bearing date the thirty-first day of October
in the year of our Lord one thousand seven hundred and fifty
four and of his reign the twenty eight establishing the said college, it is among other things granted that the Governors of the
College of the Province of New York in the City of New York
in America to and for the use of the said college shall and may
have full power and authority to give, grant, bargain, sell,

demise, assign or otherwise dispose of all or any messuages, lands, tenements, rents and other hereditaments and real estate, and all goods chattels money and other things whatsoever as to them shall seem fit either in the payment of the salary or salaries of the president, fellows and professors of the said College or any other officers or ministers of the same at their will and pleasure (except as therein is excepted) 𝖆𝖓𝖉 𝖜𝖍𝖊𝖗𝖊𝖆𝖘 some doubts have arose whether the said corporation have by reason of the above in part recited clause of the said charter, power in any manner to dispose of any their messuages, lands, tenements, rents, hereditaments or real estate not comprised within the said exception unless in the payment of the salary or salaries aforesaid. Now for preventing all doubts or disputes concerning the same for the future, we do by these presents for us, our heirs, and successors of our especial grace certain knowledge and mere motion ordain and declare and give and grant to the Governors of the College of the Province of New York in the city of New York in America and their successors for ever that it shall and may be lawfull for them and their successors for ever by the same name, to give, grant, bargain, sell, demise, assign or otherwise dispose of the lands, tenements and hereditaments by these presents granted, and all other the messuages, lands, tenements, rents, and other hereditaments and real estate which they now or hereafter may have or hold (not comprised within the said exception) either in fee simple, for life or lives or for years, or in any other manner whatsoever which they shall think most conducive to the benefit of the said College, any thing in the said charter above mentioned to the contrary thereof in any wise notwithstanding. 𝕬𝖓𝖉 𝖜𝖍𝖊𝖗𝖊𝖆𝖘 the said exception in the said charter above mentioned respects certain lands in the said charter more particularly described, situate on the west side of the broad way in the West ward of the City of New York which at the time of granting the said charter were set apart and have been since conveyed by the rector and inhabitants of the City of New York in communion of the Church of England as by law established to the Governors of the College of the Province of New York in the city of New York in America in fee to and for the use of the said College and it is thereby ordained that no grant or lease of the said land or any part thereof shall be made by the said governors of the said college which shall exceed the number of twenty-one years and that either in possession, or not above three years before the end and expiration or determination of the estate or estates in possession as by the same charter recourse being thereunto had, may more fully appear. 𝔄𝔫𝔡 𝔴𝔥𝔢𝔯𝔢𝔞𝔰 the Governors of the College of the Province of New York of the city of New York in America by their farther humble petition presented unto our said lieutenant governor and commander in chief of our said Province and read in our said Council for our said Province on the fourteenth day of February now last past did represent that they found the said restriction last mentioned to be prejudicial to the interest of the said college, as from the steepness of the banks of the necessity of wharfs and other impediments, that part of the said land (contained within the said exception) which fronts the North river cannot be improved but at a very great expense and therefore humbly prayed our said Lieutenant governor and commander in chief would be favorably pleased by our letters patent to enable the petitioners to grant and demise that part of the said lands which fronts the said North river to the extent of two hundred feet from the same, for any term not exceeding ninety nine years. . 𝔎𝔫𝔬𝔴 𝔶𝔢 further therefore that of our especial grace certain knowledge and mere motion, we have given and granted and by these presents for us, our heirs and successors do give and grant to the Governors of the College of the Province of New York in the city of New York in America and their successors for ever full power and authority and that it shall and may be lawful for them and their successors for ever to grant and demise for and during any term not exceeding ninety nine years, ALL THAT part and parcel of the said lands (conveyed as aforesaid by the rector and inhabitants of the city of New York in communion of the Church of England, as by law established to the said governors of the college of the Province of New York in the city of New York in America) from the whole front thereof on the said North river as far back as the depth of two hundred feet from the said river, anything in the said charter contained to the contrary thereof in any wise notwithstanding. AND WE do moreover of our especial grace and certain knowledge and mere motion, consent and agree, that this our present grant being registered, recorded and a doquet thereof made as before directed and appointed shall be good and effectual in the law to all intents, constructions and purposes whatsoever against us, our heirs and successors notwithstanding any misreciting, misbounding, misnaming or other imperfections or omission of in or in any wise concerning the above granted or hereby mentioned or intended to be granted lands, tenements, hereditaments, powers, privileges, authorities and premises or any part thereof.

𝔍n testimony whereof we have caused these our letters to be made patent and the great seal of our said Province to be hereunto affixed. 𝔚itness our said trusty and well beloved Cadwallader Colden, Esquire, our said lieutenant governor and commander in chief of our said Province of New York and the territories depending thereon in America at our Fort in our city of New York by and with the advice and consent of our said Council for our said Province the fourteenth day of March in the year of our Lord one thousand seven hundred and seventy and of our reign the tenth.

CLARKE.

[GREAT SEAL OF THE PROVINCE.]

First Skin Line the fortieth the letter *a* is interlined; and Second Skin Line the forty-third part of the word *be* wrote in erasure.

(Endorsed):

New York Secretary's Office 22 March 1770 The within Letters Patent are recorded in this Office in Lib. Patents No 15 page 72 &c

GEO. BANYAR
D. Sec'y

New York Auditor General's Office 23 March 1770. The within Letters Patent are Docqueted in this Office

GEO. BANYAR
Dep. Aud$^{r.}$

LEASE OF LAND IN THE TOWNSHIP OF NORBURY.

𝕿𝖍𝖎𝖘 𝕴𝖓𝖉𝖊𝖓𝖙𝖚𝖗𝖊, made the Sixth Day of April in the year of
our Lord One thousand seven hundred and Seventy four BE-
TWEEN His Excellency William Tryon Esquire Captain General
and Governor in Chief in and over the Province of New York in
America of the one Part and the Governors of the College of
the Province of New York in the City of New York in America
of the other Part 𝖂𝖎𝖙𝖓𝖊𝖘𝖘𝖊𝖙𝖍 That His said Excellency William
Tryon for and in Consideration of the Sum of Five Shillings of
lawful money of the Province of New York to him in Hand paid
by the said Parties of the second Part the Receipt whereof is
hereby acknowledged HATH granted bargained and sold and by
these Presents DOTH grant bargain and sell unto the said Governors of the College of the Province of New York in the
City of New York in America 𝕬𝖑𝖑 𝖙𝖍𝖆𝖙 certain Tract or Parcel of
Land Situate lying and being in the County of Gloucester in the
Province of New York being the Northwesterly Part of a certain
Tract of Land containing Thirty Thousand Acres and the usual
Allowance for Highways granted unto Samuel Chandler and
others by Letters Patent under the Great Seal of the Province
of New York bearing Date the Fourteenth Day of April in the
Year of our Lord One thousand seven hundred and Seventy two
and erected into a Township by the Name of NORBURY, The
same Tract or Parcel of Land by these Presents intended to be
granted BEGINNING at the most Westerly Corner of the said
Township of Norbury Thence running along the Southwesterly
Bounds of the said Township South Sixty Degrees East Two
hundred and Twenty Chains; Thence North Thirty Degrees
East to the Northeasterly Bounds of the said Township Thence
along the last mentioned Bounds North Sixty Degrees West to
the most Northerly Corner of the said Township; Thence
along Northwesterly Bounds of the said Township, to the
Place of beginning above mentioned Containing Ten thousand
Acres of Land and the usual Allowance for Highways, TOGETHER
with all and Singular the Emoluments Hereditaments and Appurtenances to the same and every Part and Parcel thereof belonging or in anywise appertaining AND the Reversion and

Reversions, Remainder and Remainders Rents Issues and Profits thereof and of every Part and Parcel thereof with their and every of their appurtenances 𝔱𝔬 𝔥𝔞𝔳𝔢 𝔞𝔫𝔡 𝔱𝔬 𝔥𝔬𝔩𝔡 all and Singular the said Tract of Ten thousand Acres of Land and the usual Allowance for Highways and other the Premises hereby bargained and sold and every Part and Parcel thereof with their and every of their appurtenances unto the said Governors of the College of the Province of New York in the City of New York in America and their Successors and Assigns from the Day next before the Day of the Date of these Presents for and during and unto the full End and Term of one whole Year from thence next ensuing and fully to be compleat and ended YIELDING AND PAYING therefore at the Expiration of the said Year one Pepper Corn if the same shall be lawfully demanded TO the Intent and Purpose that by Virtue of these Presents and of the Statute for Transferring Uses into Possession they the said Governors of the College of the Province of New York in the City of New York in America may be in the actual Possession of all and Singular the Premises hereby bargained and sold with the Appurtenances and thereby be enabled to accept and take a Grant and Release of the Reversion and Inheritance thereof to them and their Successors To the only proper Use and Behoof of them the said Governors of the College of the Province of New York in the City of New York in America their Successors and Assigns for ever to for and upon such Intents and Purposes as shall be thereof declared.

𝕴𝖓 𝖜𝖎𝖙𝖓𝖊𝖘𝖘 whereof his said Excellency has to one Part of these Indentures set his Hand and Seal and to the other Part thereof the said Governors of the College of the Province of New York in the City of New York in America have caused their Common Seal to be affixed the Day and Year first above written.

WM. (Seal) TRYON.

(Endorsed.)

SEALED and Delivered in the Presence of ⎫
  (Line four and Ten Razures filled up ⎬
  and Line Sixteen the word *Successors* ⎪
  wrote on Razure.) ⎭

PETER OGILVIE,
WM. BANYAR.

RELEASE OF LAND IN THE TOWNSHIP OF NORBURY.

𝕿𝖍𝖎𝖘 𝕴𝖓𝖉𝖊𝖓𝖙𝖚𝖗𝖊 made the Seventh Day of April in the Year of our Lord One Thousand Seven Hundred and Seventy four BETWEEN his Excellency William Tryon Esquire Governor in chief in and over the Province of New York in AMERICA of the one Part and the Governors of the College of the Province of New York in the City of New York in AMERICA of the other Part 𝖂𝖎𝖙𝖓𝖊𝖘𝖘𝖊𝖙𝖍 That his said Excellency William Tryon for the Esteem which he bears to the said College and from a Desire of advancing as well the Interests thereof as to promote and extend its Usefullness in disseminating the Principles of Virtue, Literature and Loyalty and also for and in Consideration of the Sum of Five Shillings of lawful Money of the Province of New York to him in Hand paid by the said Parties of the second Part the Receipt whereof is hereby acknowledged HATH granted aliened released conveyed and confirmed and by these Presents DOTH clearly and absolutely grant alien release convey and confirm unto the said Governors of the College of the Province of New York in the City of New York in America (in their actual Possession now being by Virtue of a Lease to them thereof made for one whole Year by Indenture bearing Date the Day next before the Day of the Date of these Presents and by Force of the Statute for Transferring Uses into Possession) and to their Successors and Assigns for ever 𝕬𝖑𝖑 𝖙𝖍𝖆𝖙 certain Tract or Parcel of Land situate lying and being in the County of Gloucester in the Province of New York being the Northwesterly part of a certain Tract of Land containing Thirty Thousand Acres and the several Allowances for Highways granted unto Samuel Chandler and others by Letters Patent under the Great Seal of the Province of New York bearing Date the Fourteenth Day of April in the Year of our Lord One thousand Seven hundred and Seventy two and erected into a Township by the name of NORBURY The same Tract or Parcel of Land by these Presents intended to be granted Beginning at the Most Westerly

Corner of the Township of Norbury thence running along the
Southwesterly Bounds of the said Township South Sixty De-
grees East Two hundred and Twenty Chains, thence North
Thirty Degrees East to the northeasterly Bounds of the said
Township Thence along the last mentioned Bounds North Sixty
Degrees West to the most northerly Corner of the said Town-
ship Thence along the Northwesterly Bounds of the said Town-
ship to the Place of Beginning above mentioned containing
Ten Thousand Acres of Land and the usual Allowance for
Highways TOGETHER with all and singular the Emoluments and
Hereditaments and Appurtenances to the same and every part
and parcel thereof belonging or in anywise appertaining And
the Reversion and Reversions Remainder and Remainders
Rents Issues and Profits thereof and of every Part and Parcel
thereof with their and every of their Appurtenances and also all
the Estate Right, Title, Interest, Claim and Demand whatsoever in Law and Equity of him the said William Tryon of in
and to the same and to every Part and Parcel thereof with the
Appurtenances to have and to hold all and singular the said
Tract of Ten Thousand Acres of Land and the usual Allowance
for Highways and other the Premises hereby granted and every
Part and Parcel thereof with their and every of their Appurtenances unto the said Governors of the College of the Province
of New York in the City of New York in AMERICA and their
Successors and Assigns for Ever To the only proper Use
and Behoof of the said Governors of the College of the Province
of New York in the City of New York in AMERICA and their
Successors and Assigns for Ever To the End and Purpose and
upon this special Trust and Confidence nevertheless that they
the said Governors of the College of the Province of New York
in the City of New York in AMERICA and their Successors
for ever Whether the said Corporation shall continue to be
called by the Name or Title aforesaid or by any other
Name or Stile whatsoever do and shall well and faithfully grant in Fee Farm or from Time to Time demise and
let the Lands hereby granted for such Term and Terms of
Years and to such Person or Persons in such Parts and Par-
cels and on such Terms Conditions and Rents as they shall
judge most advantageous for increasing the annual Profits

thereof to the said Corporation and that they and their Successors from Time to Time when and as the Rents Issues and * *
Profits aforesaid shall become sufficient for the Support and
Maintenance thereof do establish One or more Professorship or
Professorships of and in the said Seminary in such Branch or
Branches of Literature as to the said Corporation shall seem
expedient and that they from Time to Time increase the Number of Professorships as the Funds which shall arise from the
said Lands as aforesaid shall become capable of decently supporting the Professor so to be appointed And upon this further
especial Trust and Confidence that the said Corporation from
Time to Time do well and faithfully apply in Stipends to such
Professor or Professors all and singular the clear Rents Issues
and Profits aforesaid after deducting the necessary Costs
Charges and Expences attending the Management or Preservation of the said Lands and Premises hereby granted and all other
Charges and Expences which the said Corporation shall in any
manner become liable to pay for or on Account of the said Lands
and Premises. Always provided that when at any Time or
Times hereafter the clear annual Rents Issues and Profits aforesaid shall in the Judgment of the said Corporation be more than
sufficient to support any certain Number of Professorships and
not sufficient to support one more Professorship that it shall be
lawfull for them to retain such Overplus and put the same at
Interest for the Increase of the said Fund the same Interest to be
nevertheless applied together with the Annual Overplus aforesaid (when the same shall be sufficient) for the Support of
another Professorship ALL and Singular which said Professors
to be appointed by the said Corporation in Manner and Form as
other Professors in the said Seminary are directed to be
appointed by the present Charter of the said Corporation or
in such other Manner and Form as Professors in the said
Seminary shall or may be hereafter directed to be appointed by
any other Charter or Charters hereafter to be granted to the said
Corporation and subject to all and singular the Regulations
Rules and Orders which the said Corporation already hath or
shall from Time to Time think fit to make for the Regulation of
their Professors in general or for the particular Regulation and
Government of the Professors to be supported as aforesaid The

said Professors when established according to the true Intent and Meaning of these Presents to be severally called and known by the Name of TRYONIAN PROFESSORS the first Professor so to be appointed to be a Professor of the municipal Laws of England.

In witness whereof his said Excellency has to one part of these Presents set his Hand and Seal and to the other part thereof the said Governors of the College of the Province of New York in the City of New York in AMERICA have caused their Common Seal to be affixed the Day and Year first above written.

WM. (seal) TRYON.

(Endorsed)

SEALED AND DELIVERED in the Presence of ⎫
   Line Sixteen the Words *and Assigns* wrote ⎪
   on Razure and Line Seventeen a Rasure ⎬
   filled up and Line Twenty five the word ⎪
   not interlined ⎭

PETER OGILVIE
WM. BANYAR.

Charters of Alumni Associations.

ASSOCIATION OF THE ALUMNI OF COLUMBIA COLLEGE.

An Act to incorporate "The Association of the Alumni of Columbia College." Passed May 21st, 1874. Laws of 1874, Chapter 520.

The People of the State of New York, represented in Senate and Assembly, do enact as follows :

Section 1. Henry Drisler, Frederic De Peyster, J. Howard Van Amringe, Charles R. Swords, Henry James Anderson, William Mitchell, George P. Quackenbos, Charles A. Silliman, William H. Butterworth, Joseph B. Lawrence, Henry R. Beekman, William Bayard Cutting, James McNamee, James M. Brady, Seth Low, and Stuyvesant Fish, at present forming the officers and standing committee of "The Association of the Alumni of Columbia College," together with such other persons as appear to be members of that association on the books of the treasurer of the same, and not to be in arrears more than two years for dues, and also with such other persons as shall hereafter become members of the corporation hereby created in such manner and upon such terms as shall be prescribed in the constitution or by-laws of such corporation, are hereby constituted and created a body corporate and politic in fact and in name by the name of "The Association of the Alumni of Columbia College," for the purposes mentioned in this act; and by that name they, and their successors and associates, shall have perpetual succession, and shall be capable in law of suing and being sued, and of receiving, purchasing, holding, conveying, leasing, mortgaging, or otherwise disposing of any real and personal estate for the use and benefit of said corporation, which estate shall not exceed the net annual income of twenty thousand dollars.

Sec. 2. The object of this corporation shall be to perpetuate the friendships and relations arising during the course of study in Columbia College, to promote the true interests, influence and efficiency of Columbia College as an institution of sound learning and practical education, and with these objects to establish lectureships, to have meetings of the members of said corporation for social and literary purposes and for the management of its business, to appoint from time to time (if the trustees of Columbia College shall consent thereto, and with such restrictions, if any, as said trustees shall prescribe) such number of trustees of said college as said college may, by general rules, or from time to time, authorize said corporation hereby constituted to appoint.

SEC. 3. The said corporation, at one or more special meetings to be called by its standing committee for that purpose, shall have power to frame its constitution and by-laws, with provisions therein for subsequent amendments of the same, provided the said constitution, by-laws and amendments be not inconsisent with the laws or constitution of the United States or of this State, and that there be present at such special meeting at least thirty members.

SEC. 4. The officers of said corporation shall be, until otherwise prescribed by their constitution, a president, vice-president, secretary, and treasurer, who, with twelve other members to be elected at a general or special meeting shall be the standing committee of said corporation.

SEC. 5. Such standing committee shall have such powers as shall be lawfully conferred on them by the constitution and by-laws of the corporation, and they and the said officers shall hold their offices for such time and in such manner as such constitution and by-laws shall prescribe.

SEC. 6. Such constitution and by-laws may declare what number of members shall constitute a quorum at meetings of the standing committee, and provide for the manner of admitting and suspending and removing members and officers of the corporation.

SEC. 7. The said corporation shall be subject to and have the rights conferred by the general provisions contained in the third title of the eighteenth chapter of the first part of the Revised Statutes, except that no member of said corporation shall be liable for any debts or liabilities of the same unless on an agreement in writing to be subscribed by such member and expressly binding him.

SEC. 8. The said corporation, hereby constituted, may take real and personal estate by will, but subject to the general provisions of the act relating to wills, passed April thirteenth, eighteen hundred and sixty, chapter three hundred and sixty.

SEC. 9. The several officers of said association existing at the time of the passage of this act, shall hold their respective offices as officers of this corporation with the powers and duties pre-scribed by the constitution and by-laws of said association until their successors shall be elected or appointed. Further, all property, rights and interests of said association shall by virtue of this act vest in and become the property of this corporation.

SEC. 10. All interest of any member of said corporation in its property shall terminate and vest in the corporation upon his ceasing to be a member thereof by death, resignation, expulsion or otherwise.

SEC. 11. The Legislature may at any time alter, amend, or repeal this act.

SEC. 12. This act shall take effect immediately.

THE ASSOCIATION OF THE ALUMNI

OF THE

COLLEGE OF PHYSICIANS AND SURGEONS

IN THE CITY OF NEW YORK.

CERTIFICATE OF INCORPORATION.

STATE OF NEW YORK, } ss:
City and County of New York. }

We, the undersigned, members of "THE ASSOCIATION OF THE ALUMNI OF THE COLLEGE OF PHYSICIANS AND SURGEONS IN THE CITY OF NEW YORK," of which Cornelius R. Agnew is President; Robert A. Barry, Vice-President; Frederick A. Burrall, Secretary; George Bayles, Assistant Secretary; and Timothy M. Cheesman, Treasurer, and all other members of said Association and Alumni of said College, who may now be or hereafter become associated with us, do by these presents, pursuant to and in compliance with the Act of the Legislature of the State of New York, passed on the twelfth day of April, one thousand eight hundred and forty-eight, entitled "An Act for the Incorporation of Benevolent, Charitable, Scientific and Missionary Societies," and the several acts of the Legislature amendatory thereof, associate ourselves together and form a body politic and corporate, and do hereby certify:

FIRST. That the corporate name of said Association is: "THE ASSOCIATION OF THE ALUMNI OF THE COLLEGE OF PHYSICIANS AND SURGEONS IN THE CITY OF NEW YORK."

SECOND. That the objects for which the said Corporation is formed are: the collection of funds by contribution and subscription, and the holding, investment and application of the same for the establishment and endowment of professorships and fellowships, the creation of prize funds, the establishment and equipment of laboratories, the erection and equipment of suitable buildings for the same, or the alteration and repair of buildings already erected, and for the purpose of buying, holding, and hiring, or leasing property for any and such other

91

purposes of medical and scientific investigation and instruction, in connection and co-operation with the Trustees of the "COLLEGE OF PHYSICIANS AND SURGEONS IN THE CITY OF NEW YORK," as the said "ASSOCIATION OF THE ALUMNI" of said College, in pursuance of its Constitution and By-Laws, may direct.

THIRD.   That the number of Trustees of said Corporation shall be five, whose names are as follows: Gurdon Buck, M.D.; D. Tilden Brown, M.D.; Robert A. Barry, M.D.; Henry C. Eno, M.D.; Thomas E. Satterthwaite, M.D.; and who shall manage the concerns of the Corporation for the first year.

(Signed)   GURDON BUCK, M.D.
D. TILDEN BROWN, M.D.
ROBERT A. BARRY, M.D.
HENRY C. ENO, M.D.
THOMAS E. SATTERTHWAITE, M.D.

STATE OF NEW YORK, ⎫
City and County of New York, ⎬ ss :

On this 5th day of May, A.D. 1873, before me personally appeared Gurdon Buck, M.D., D. Tilden Brown, M.D., Robert A. Barry, M.D., Henry C. Eno, M.D., and Thomas E. Satterthwaite, M.D., to me known to be the individuals described in the foregoing certificate, and they severally before me signed the said certificate and acknowledged that they signed the certificate for the purpose therein mentioned.

WILLIAM J. BELL,
Notary Public,
N. Y. County.

(Endorsed)

I, one of the Justices of the Supreme Court of the State of New York, in the First Judicial District, hereby approve of the within certificate and consent that the same be filed.

May 12th, 1873.   E. L. FANCHER,
J. S. C.

Filed in the office of the Clerk of the County of New York, on the 12th day of May, and in the office of the Secretary of State at Albany, on the 13th day of May, 1873.

THE ASSOCIATION OF THE ALUMNI

SCHOOL OF MINES OF COLUMBIA COLLEGE.

CERTIFICATE OF INCORPORATION.

STATE OF NEW YORK, ⎫ ss:
City and County of New York, ⎭

We, the undersigned, Frederick Augustus Schermerhorn, John Krom Rees, Pierre de Peyster Ricketts, Frederick Remsen Hutton, John C. Fitz Randolph, and Alfred Joseph Moses desiring to form a society or club pursuant to the provisions of an act passed by the Legislature of the State of N. Y., May 12, 1875, and entitled "An Act for the incorporation of societies or clubs for certain lawful purposes" and of the several acts extending and amending the same, do hereby certify:

That the name or title by which such society shall be known in law is " THE ASSOCIATION OF THE ALUMNI OF THE SCHOOL OF MINES OF COLUMBIA COLLEGE."

That the particular business and object of such society is to promote the professional welfare of its members, and to strengthen the bonds of professional and social fellowship between the Alumni of the School of Mines.

That the number of managers who shall manage the concerns of said society are twelve.

That the names of the managers for the first year are: Frederick Augustus Schermerhorn, John Krom Rees, Pierre de Peyster Ricketts, Frederick Remsen Hutton, John C. Fitz Randolph, Alfred Joseph Moses, John Henry Banks, Willard Parker Butler, Peter Townsend Austen, Nathaniel Low Britton, Alfred Lockwood Beebe, James Furman Kemp.

That a majority of the managers are citizens of the State of New York.

That the principal office of such society shall be situated in the City, County and State of New York.

IN WITNESS WHEREOF we have hereunto set our hands this twentieth day of May 1886

> F. AUG SCHERMERHORN
> JOHN KROM REES
> PIERRE DE PEYSTER RICKETTS
> FREDERICK REMSEN HUTTON
> JOHN C. F. RANDOLPH
> ALFRED JOSEPH MOSES

STATE OF NEW YORK, ⎫ ss:—
City and County of New York. ⎬

On the twentieth day of May 1886 before me personally came John Krom Rees, Pierre de Peyster Ricketts, Alfred Joseph Moses and Frederick Remsen Hutton; on the 24th day of May 1886 before me personally came John C. F. Randolph and on the 25th day of May 1886 before me personally came Frederick Augustus Schermerhorn, all of whom are to me known and known to me to be the individuals described in and who executed the foregoing certificate, and they severally before me signed the said certificate and acknowledged that they executed the same.

WITNESS my hand and official seal this 25th day of May, 1886.

[L. S.]   EDWIN T. RICE, JR.
                              Notary Public (54)
                              N. Y. Co.

I, CHARLES DONOHUE, a Justice of the Supreme Court of the State of New York in and for the First Judicial District, in which district the principal office of the Association of the Alumni of the School of Mines of Columbia College shall be located, do hereby approve of the foregoing Certificate of Incorporation, and consent that the same be filed.

Dated New York May 28, 1886.

                              C. DONOHUE.

Filed and recorded in the office of the County Clerk June 8, 1886.

www.ingramcontent.com/pod-product-compliance
Lightning Source LLC
Chambersburg PA
CBHW031438270326
41930CB00007B/766